ZOLA LEVITT

Some Of My Best Friends Are Christians

A Division of G/L Publications
Glendale, California, U.S.A.

G/L REGAL BOOKS

Other good Regal reading:
*What's a Nice Jewish Boy Like You Doing in the
    First Baptist Church?* by Bob Friedman
Pursued by Vera Schlamm with Bob Friedman
Inside Jerusalem, City of Destiny by Arnold Olson
What More Can God Say? by Ray C. Stedman

Scripture quotations in this publication are from the
Authorized King James Version and from the *New American
Standard Bible.* © The Lockman Foundation 1960, 1962,
1963, 1968, 1971. Used by permission.

Published by Regal Books Division, G/L Publications
Glendale, California 91209
Printed in U.S.A.

Library of Congress Catalog Card No. 77-90581
ISBN 0-8307-0591-0

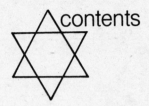

contents

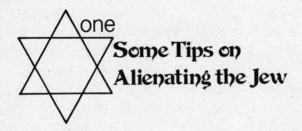

one
Some Tips on Alienating the Jew

My father never liked the Gentiles. Something about the *goyim* turned him off.

And he brought me up to think the same way. "Show me a Gentile and I'll show you a guy who has something against the Jews," he used to preach to me. The very sight of somebody ordering ham and cheese on white with mayonnaise was enough to make my father drop his corned beef sandwich (on rye with mustard) and run for his life.

The fact is, to give my father his due, he *did* have to run for his life, with the Gentiles in hot pursuit, back in the old country. He was entitled to his aversion. He came by it honestly.

But I never really went along with his philosophy.

7

I discovered some nice people who weren't Jewish—virtually an impossibility in my father's mind—and I liked hanging around with them. They didn't seem as smart or as funny as my Jewish buddies but they had their good points all the same. They could fight better, for one thing. (Oh, if only the Israelites had been real fighters, world history would read a lot different. Instead they have always been the world's pushovers.) And they were good at sports, where few Jewish people have really excelled.

Finally I discovered some really nice Gentiles, but they weren't Gentiles anymore. They were Christians, which, I found, was slightly different.

I got to be 32 years old by the time I discovered Christians, or until they got around to discovering *me*. They never did discover my father; he lived 70 years among Christians up and down the block who never mentioned the Messiah to him, and he's gone on now to whatever his reward might be.

I'm going to give my testimony, my own experience with the Jewish Messiah, in the next chapter. But suffice it here to say that these wonderfully peaceful and spiritual former Gentiles I met struck me as having one outstanding omission in their otherwise zealous service of the Lord: *They had completely forgotten about my people.*

As devoted as they all seemed to be to the Jewish Messiah; as faithfully as they studied their Old and New Testaments, written and published by Jews; as admiring as they were of those courageous first century disciples and apostles, all Jews, who built the

Christian church to begin with; they seemed to utterly disregard the Jews.

I was a believer for more than a year before I discovered that there was such a thing as a mission to the Jews. I went from church to church without seeing a single Jew. There seemed to be an unwritten law that the Jews weren't supposed to come to church at all. (Actually, under Edward I in England a few centuries ago that was a *written law*.)

But the way *I* read the gospel, it was all about the Jews. My copy of Matthew has the Lord Himself saying, "I am not sent but unto the lost sheep of the house of Israel" (15:24). Jeremiah, whose magnificent writings I studied in Hebrew school as a boy, prophesied about the advent of Christianity this way: "I will make a new covenant with the house of Israel, and with the house of Judah" (31:31). I have a copy of a letter written to the Romans by one of my favorite rabbis, Paul. He says that the gospel is supposed to go to my people *first* (1:16). That worthy Jewish scholar went on to say, "Brethren, my heart's desire and prayer to God for Israel is, that they might be saved" (10:1), and, "Hath God cast away his people? God forbid!" (11:1).

What in the world is going on here?

Why aren't Christians witnessing to the Jews?

Some of My Best Friends . . .

I think Christians don't witness to the Jews because they don't know the Jews very well.

Christians are funny people. They'll gladly witness

9

to the folks at the office and the people on the block, and they'll gladly go to New Guinea and witness to headhunters. But it seems like they don't bother with anybody in between.

Christians will patiently dry out drunken derelicts fresh from the gutters and feed them soup and the gospel. They'll learn the languages of stone-age islanders and travel 10,000 miles to tell them about salvation and to translate the New Testament into their obscure tongues. They'll slip behind the Iron Curtain, on pain of death, and rally the oppressed unfortunates with the hopeful message of Christ.

But the simple task of walking across the street to the home of the local Jew, who already believes in God and speaks English, seems beyond the Christian church.

Part of not knowing the Jew very well is evidenced by the Christian's idea that the Jew will automatically resent hearing about salvation. Christians think they'll insult their Jewish friends by discussing the gospel. "I have a good relationship with Feinberg and he's a nice guy. Why should I double-cross him by forcing my religion on him?" The social objections are legion. "It's not that I don't like the Jews, of course. After all, some of my best friends—"

Jesus' best friends were Jews and He laid down His life for His friends.

If a Christian *really* believes the message of salvation, including the part about hell being reserved for those who don't have it, he won't try to say that he'd rather not witness to his friends. If you like Feinberg, try to take him to the Kingdom with you. If you don't, you're going to miss him when his Messiah returns. Believe me, you won't enjoy the Kingdom of God without Jews in it. And God never intended to leave them out anyway.

Gentiles tend to hang around with Gentiles. "Church fellowship" means that a group of Gentiles who like each other have get-togethers. The Lord dealt with that: "And if you greet your brothers only, what do you do more than others? Do not even the Gentiles do the same?" (Matt. 5:47, *NASB*).

The Crusader Syndrome

Ever since those Crusaders came to Israel with their long knives, Jews haven't been wild about Christian crusades. "This Crusade for Christ," and "That Crusade for Christ" have as much appeal for the Jew as taking an Arab to lunch.

There are wonderful ways of approaching the Jewish people on behalf of their Messiah and I'm going to disclose a lot of them in this little book, but first I'd like to make very clear just how the Jews get turned off. I want to use this first chapter for some tips on alienating the Jew.

The truth is, the church has been alienating the Jew for centuries, and when the Lord asks, "How did you treat my brothers?" (See Matt. 25:40-46) there's going to be some embarrassment. Things need to turn around, and pretty quickly, if we are to understand that the Lord wants some results among His people.

Now the Jew is easy to insult, I must admit, and

11

most alienation of the Jew is unconscious. Christians today, at least Bible-reading Christians, don't want to turn *anybody* off, and least of all not the "chosen people." But it's been happening all the same, and I have an idea or two about what's been going on.

It should be understood that the matters which follow, in fact this whole book, boils down to one Jew's opinion. I'm not really a scholar of these things and I don't bring a dozen Jews a day to the Lord. But I did practice Judaism for most of my life, at least in the form we find it in the Jewish community today, and I did get a pretty good picture of what we found so irksome about the Gentiles, Christian and otherwise.

And now that I've found the Lord I think every Jew should meet Him and I want to help out.

"Choose Somebody Else for Awhile"

I quote Tevye, the hero of "Fiddler on the Roof," in a lot of my books and I must apologize to regular readers for a certain amount of unavoidable repetition on topics Jewish in general. We have really only a paltry number of Jews in the world, relatively speaking, and only one Lord. Bringing them together doesn't involve that many different formulas. So if I say something I've told you before, please forgive.

Tevye said a mouthful to God when discussing his own status as a chosen person. He told God patiently that he deeply appreciated the fact that the Jews were the chosen people, but in view of all that that distinction involved he thought he had to make one

heartfelt request: "Choose somebody else for awhile."

And there lies a rub. Would you believe that it gets a little tiresome to be the chosen people?

Yes, we were chosen to have a land, to be a blessing to the world, to be miraculously delivered from slavery, to get the law, to hear the prophets, to receive the Messiah, etc., etc. But we have also been chosen by the Nazis, the Russians and seemingly everybody else looking for a people to lean on. The Bible tells of ages and ages of persecution of the Jews by other nations, and that was only the *good* 2,000 years. That we have a destiny with God we enjoy contemplating. But it's obvious that Satan chose us as soon as God chose us.

To some Jews the situation is almost like one of those good-news-bad-news jokes. God says, "Congratulations, I choose you as My people . . . now let me introduce my servant Nebuchadnezzar."

I heard a sermon in a synagogue where the rabbi was talking about contemporary Judaism. His topic was the novelist Philip Roth. He quoted a Yiddish proverb which boiled down to, "It's tough to be Jewish." But what Roth had written indicated a new question to the rabbi. "Granted, it's tough to be Jewish," he preached, "but does it have to be *sick* to be Jewish?"

Being Jewish is *so* special that it sometimes becomes a liability.

And there's the turn-off. The Jew doesn't care to be told, on and on, that he belongs to some abnormal category of the human race.

14

We're not from outer space, after all. We eat, breathe and reproduce the same way as everybody else. We are neither subhuman, as the Nazis thought, nor superhuman, as some believers seem to think.

You should be around to see some of the phony smiles and knuckle-cracking handshakes I have to endure at each new church where I speak. (First, of course, I get examined in a sort of deleterious way— "That fella wears a beard; well, I guess they're all like that.") I was invited to be baptized at a church once because, "our people would sure get a kick out of seeing one of *you folks* baptized." He almost gave me a conspiratorial wink.

Somehow I get the same feeling the blacks must get when somebody gives them that, "Hi there, Jackson. I want you to know we're *especially* glad to have *you* on the team." I don't want to be thought of as a weirdo, but being chosen can. work against me.

We Jews don't want to feel quite that special. Somehow we feel "put in their place" by an overdone respect for our differences and our supposed special "in" with God. It would be better for serious Bible students to check out exactly what the Jews were chosen *for*, and then act accordingly.

If we look at Genesis 12:1-3 we can read the Abrahamic covenant, God's original contract with the Jewish people, and see exactly what the choice of the Jews was all about. The Jews were to have a *land*, they were to be a *blessing* to all nations, and they were to be a kind of *measuring stick* for other peoples ("I will bless them that bless thee, and curse him that curseth thee."). And that's the long and short of it. God enhanced the covenant considerably, making it more definite, adding in the promise of the Messiah, the entire Law, the precise designation of whose descendants were to have the Promised Land (Isaac's, not Ishmael's—Gen. 17:19-21) and many other facets of this unique Father and children relationship.

But the basic covenant remained the same throughout the Scriptures, including the New Testament, and of course it remains immutable today. God promised His friend Abraham that the covenant would be in force "forever."

Now suppose we treated the chosen people according to their covenant. Suppose we emphasized only the elements that God emphasized. Rather than finding it peculiar that they cover their heads when they pray, cure colds with chicken soup, tell jokes nobody else thinks are funny and take odd days off all year, what would happen if we stuck to God's original terms?

Well, then we would emphasize the land of Israel, the very first utterance of God to Abraham. We'd be very interested in this remarkable fulfillment of so much prophecy, this amazing recovery of a land by a dispersed people, unprecedented in human history. We'd be vitally interested in the progress and safety of the Promised Land.

Perhaps we wouldn't march in Zionistic parades or buy Israeli bonds, but we would be seeing an issue the way God sees it. I don't really mean to discuss politics so much as merely refer to the Scriptures. But Israel, just as it now stands—prophetically the spiritual and political center of the world—is the most vital biblical issue in the world today.

Those knowledgeable of Bible prophecy can appreciate just how it happens that little Israel, so recently come into being after so long a time, has the attention of the entire world community. In fact, those knowledgeable about end times prophecy can see ahead more clearly every day as they watch Israel.

Now, on that second point of the covenant, things get a bit more complicated.

How can you help the Jew be a blessing to you? The Jew is supposed to be a blessing to everybody.

Well, first you could get to know him. Jews make good and faithful friends, people who know Jews will tell you. While the Jews do bless the world in wonderful ways—through medicine, law, business and the other professions they invariably frequent—their special blessing is supposed to be a different thing. They're supposed to take faith to the world.

They have done that by producing the Messiah, some say, and their task is finished. They were only to be the people out of which He came. But the Jews received the Holy Spirit as well, of course (Acts 2:5), and they did share Him with the world. They built those churches you read about in the New Testament and they supplied the only Bible those churches used —the Old Testament. They sent the missionaries to tell the Gentiles of the Jewish Messiah. When God wanted to call out missionaries He called His people —Peter, Paul, John and the rest.

17

The Jews made the best missionaries the world has ever seen, and the only reason they aren't still taking the gospel to the world is that we haven't shared it with them. They are natural salesmen, anyone can see. They are gregarious, enthusiastic, influential. But since virtually nobody has witnessed to the new generations of Jews for some 19 centuries they have become salesmen without a product. Lacking the gospel they now sell garments, mortgages, jewelry and so forth. But *they were meant to sell Christ.*

If we would equip them to take the gospel to the world then we would be doing things God's way. They would be a blessing.

Even unsaved as they are, they still have those tendencies toward mission work that God built into them at the start. It's not just the salesmanship; they live decently and they are godly with the light they have. Imagine how effective they would be with the power of Christ behind them!

We are running a church without the ones God selected, and will select in the future, to do a major share of the mission work. We are running a sales organization where we keep our top talent from even entering the office to get the product.

Finally, there is that third item, God's blessings. He will bless you if you bless the Jews and He will curse you if you curse them. That's what He said in Genesis 12:3.

So, if you don't allow the Jew to play golf at your club, I'd worry about you. If you think Zionism is racism you've got some problems with God. If you think of the Jews as the opposition party to the church you're not blessing them very much.

The mentality that says the Jew is supposed to be taking over our country ("our country" being anywhere the Jew has ever been) is not for believers. We don't need to suppress the Jew. Actually we need to put his talents to work. He's nobody to be afraid of. Discipled, he would help make the church the way the apostles—saved Jews—made it in the first place.

I've challenged people to pray for the Jews with remarkable results. Enough said.

The whole subject boils down to just this: Treat the Jew like a normal person. Don't conduct an adversary relationship with the Jewish community. Stop even thinking about "Jewish characteristics" except those that God specified.

The Jews are not taking over America; they are helping to build it. The Jews are the oldest people in the world, in terms of culture, religion, language and land. And they have a lot of brains and a vigorous healthy spirit. Alienating the Jews merely makes the alienator come out on the short end of things at church, with God and in society.

On to Better Things

If that's settled, we can go on to some ideas on how to witness to the Jews.

I have a simple theory about witnessing to the Jews which I'll introduce as we go along. It will probably work in all normal cases, though some people, as with the Gentiles, won't respond to anything. We don't have to witness to every Jew, the gospel indicates. When the Lord Himself had a chance to witness to no less a personage than King Herod, "He answered him nothing" (Luke 23:8,9).

Now let me recount how I happen to be here, writing this book for you. I want to start with my own story.

I was brought to the Lord by a beautiful girl.

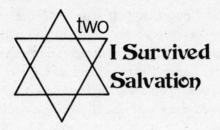

two
I Survived
Salvation

My testimony is not a case of a miracle cure from drug addiction or a rehabilitation from death row. Actually, I used to be a nominally nice guy with just normal problems and now I'm a nominally nice guy with enormous problems.

I used to just fight around with the world. Now I battle against "principalities and powers."

But it's a better life.

My story might help to shed some light on the Jewish-Gentile thing; I think I grew up in a normally contentious environment on that score. I have already indicated some essentials of my upbringing; now I'd like to fill in the details.

My books, *Confessions of a Contemporary Jew*

(Tyndale House) and *If You're There, Show Me* (Moody Press), give my story in full. But for our purposes here I'd like to contrast the Jewish and Gentile communities I experienced as I grew up. From where I stood people were gathered into very definite groups, and the life-styles of those particular groups determined their orientation to everything in life, including God.

Us and Them

I was raised on the east side of Pittsburgh where things were very ethnic. The distinct groups I remember were the blacks, the Italians-Greeks-Jews-etc., and the "regular people."

The regular people were the white Gentiles. All the rest of us were weirdos in our different ways.

Even in grade school, though, I wondered why us Jews weren't part of the regular people. I mean, the blacks were black; anybody could see that. And the Italians and Greeks, et. al., were a little strange; anybody could see that too. But we Jews were actually hard to tell apart from the regular people. We were white, after all, and we came in all sorts of complexions. My buddy Sheldon was red-headed; Donny was blond. Morty had freckles and my brother Hal was slender and handsome with a small, average looking nose. How come we were a group by ourselves?

I still don't know the answer to that, but the Jews are always a group by themselves. The answer may well go back to that covenant with Abraham; God marked out even us grade schoolers.

We were definitely the smart kids, us Jews, but that didn't make us very popular. The smartest thing to be was one of the regular people, actually, and that meant getting B's rather than A's. But I remember feeling a little proud that I was part of a group of brainy kids who were moved ahead into the next grade at some point in elementary school. I think there were 12 of us and we were all Jewish.

The black kids would beat us up a lot after school. We weren't very tough. Nobody messed around with the Italians because it was rumored that they were almost supernaturally tough, though I never saw this put to the test.

In high school the distinctions remained the same. Now the black kids were *really* tough, the Italians, etc., wore pegged pants and drove sleek cars with dual exhausts and us Jews still stuck to our books. Meanwhile, the regular kids never fought, never wore "cool" clothes, never went to the poolroom, never got in trouble with the teachers, kept making their B's and were always the top of our local society. That was just understood.

The regular kids were in charge of the school yearbook, the clean-cut activities like hall patrol, cafeteria squad and the drama group, and the fraternities and sororities. There were no fraternities and sororities for anybody else and the regular kids didn't accept any of us weirdos.

There was a certain amount of spillover, of course. Some Jewish kids made it onto the yearbook staff by wearing the "nice slacks" and button-down shirts of the regular kids, and some Jewish kids made the pegged-pants-and-poolroom-scene with the Italians. The blacks never made it anywhere except for an occasional light-skinned and friendly type about whom it was invariably said, "You know, Russell is really a pretty nice guy even though—"

The Jewish kids populated the orchestra, the heavy academic courses and the college-prep type lectures and programs. Sports were entirely the province of the regular kids; even though the blacks were demonstrably fine athletes nobody wanted them around the locker room and they tended to play their own games after school. We've profited greatly today by getting rid of *that* tradition!

The girls had sexual reputations exactly in keeping with their various groups. The regular girls were considered asexual, the Italian girls were supposed to be very fast and loose, the Jewish girls always virgins and the black girls were never mentioned. No one ever crossed the color line in those days and it was rare to even cross over the Jewish-Gentile line. Dating was largely a matter of groups, too. The Jews hung around restaurants and movies, the Italians just parked and the blacks stood on street corners down in their neighborhood. It was certainly unthinkable to bring home to one's parents a girl from another group —particularly to bring a Gentile to a Jewish home.

I always liked Gentile regular girls and it caused my father no end of grief. They varied as to keeping with their reputations, I found, and in truth all these distinctions we tended to make were very unreliable.

25

I mention all this because it serves a purpose in discussing religion. In no case, EVER, did anyone cross a religious line. No Gentile ever went to a synagogue even once where I grew up. No Jew ever went to a church. The Italians supposedly did strange and unmentionable things in their grand Catholic cathedrals and the regular people attended neat little churches with very nice lawns. The regular people, it was generally conceded, had the least laborious services and us Jews had the best deal with our many days off during the school year.

If a Gentile had approached me about Christ in those days it would have been grounds for a fight. No ifs, ands or buts. My father told me their religion was just a fake anyway and that the Jewish people had the only "real" religion.

In college, things continued along the same lines except that we had gotten rid of most of the blacks and the Italians. Now there were only two large groupings, substantially. One was the inevitable regular people who always somehow made the grade; and the other was us Jews, plugging away and getting the scholarships. Now I could belong to a fraternity because there were four Jewish fraternities at my university (and dozens of regular-peoples' fraternities).

And finally in graduate school things got down to a small smattering of good relationships and blurred distinctions. The Jews were in medicine and law, the regular people did the engineering and technical stuff, and we mixed pretty well.

Again, however, it would have been unthinkable

26

for a regular person to talk to me about Christ. (I'm sure the reader understands by now that Christ was only for the regular people. That can plainly be seen in almost any church, in fact.) I would have told my Gentile friend, "Oh, really? You can't be serious."

Of course we graduate students were quite above religion, it should be said. We were too smart for it. We were the educated elite who knew better. Some of the Jewish students still went back to the synagogue on the holidays, but mainly to emphasize their identification with Jewish culture. (Or to please their parents, who would say, "You remember my Hymie —he's in law school now. Say 'Hello' to Mr. Cohen, Hymie. He used to bounce you on his knee.")

I began to understand that some of the regular people actually took their religion seriously, but I thought it was just part of their regular-people shtick. It was "nice" to go to those neat little churches, and the regular people were and are, above all things, "nice."

I certainly didn't dream that they had anything like a valid biblical faith, and they certainly never told me so.

As a matter of fact I had gone all the way through my doctoral courses before anyone ever indicated to me that Christ was real. And that indication came forth only under duress.

It was from Yvonne, who is now my wife. I saw her at an opera audition and fell in love immediately. She was the loveliest thing I had ever seen in my entire career of investigating Gentile girls and I just had to meet her. I introduced myself and somehow talked her into having coffee with me.

She understood the whole thing as a pickup and she said, rather defensively I thought, "I try to do what Jesus tells me to do."

I had never heard it put exactly like that, I must say. I alternated between thinking she was trying to be funny or she was just insane. I told her that good-looking girls didn't need old-time religion.

We went into a sort of conversion contest where I tried to rescue her from what I thought of as narrow-mindedness and she tried to bring me to the Lord.

Now it should be understood that I didn't like "nice" people—those "regular" Gentiles I had put up with all my life. I always felt very superior to them and I detested their standoffishness and inhuman coolness. They were so reserved, so proper. But they always snubbed my people—that was part of their properness. We were more capable than they were, more competent at almost anything and more willing to mix, but they inevitably looked right past us. My addiction to their women might have been part of a perverse desire on my part to either pay them off for their stubbornness or to break through that reserve and get some passion out of them.

Yvonne dragged me to Campus Crusade for Christ meetings, which looked to me like the Kremlin of the regular people. There they were in force, with their casual just-right fashions, their pretty girls and their cool, remote mannerisms.

But somehow I enjoyed myself at those meetings.

I kept going back.

I began to see a subtle distinction between those particular Gentiles and the sort I had thought of as snobbish all my life. They were truly outgoing, though they weren't as good at it as Jews might have been. They were genuine in their way. There was a certain glow about them that I couldn't quite place.

It should not be construed that I really liked them; I just found myself somehow fascinated by them.

They were unsophisticated—"dumb" was the term I used to Yvonne. They were not very highly cultured, very brainy or very knowledgeable about anything. But I felt good around them.

I was surprised by their level of Bible study. They really seemed to dig into the Scriptures, something I had never adequately done in seven years of Hebrew school and ten years of Sunday School. And they always *applied* the Scriptures. The leader would invariably make the attempt to interpret what the Bible said in the light of everyday life. I had never come across that concept before.

And all the while Yvonne was proving out to really do "what Jesus told her to do." She was kind; she was forgiving. She testified about her faith constantly. I was deeply impressed by her.

Yvonne was a new kind of female for me. She wasn't hungry for anything, she wasn't deceptive. She had no axe to grind in this life. She wasn't particularly trying to catch a husband or avoid catching one. She didn't have strong feelings politically, which I did; she didn't care to march in demonstrations, protest injustices or fight the system. At first I thought she was just misinformed, but I finally gathered that she had somehow transcended all that. She was truly above all those things that I was constantly gnashing my teeth over. It was my first experience with a biblically spiritual person.

The King and I

Part of the rules of my seeing Yvonne were that I had to read the Bible. She refused to debate religion with me unless I did my homework.

And debate religion is about all we ever did. Yvonne wasn't about to fall for any seduction campaigns, not being in any great need of the worldly diversions. But I never thought of her as repressed; casual sex was just another hang-up she had transcended.

I was impressed by that. I had been raised in the morality of the Jewish community, where all the young women were virtuous princesses, supposedly, and something about Yvonne's calm modesty deeply appealed to me. That's not to say I didn't get turned on at times, but Yvonne kept me fed on the Word where I could see her rationale.

Well, to come to the point of all this, I met the Lord about three weeks after I met Yvonne. I read about Him in the book of John, I meditated about Him, and I finally came to the secure knowledge that He was the King. I hardly noticed that He was the King of the Jews; He just seemed to be *my* King.

The folks at Campus Crusade were delighted, of

31

course, and I suppose a little surprised. Like most Christians they imagined that Jews never come to Christ, or at least that it is inexorably difficult to bring one into the fold. But they were kind enough to accept my salvation as merely another act of God, and they were quite used to seeing God act in wonderful ways. They didn't parade me around in front of anybody or try to make a point of their special accomplishment.

I suddenly got tired of my work at the university and my doctoral progress. I was writing news releases for the university news bureau and I had completed the course-work for the doctorate but it somehow started to seem very pointless. Considering the King was coming and so many people were not ready for that, I realized that there was much more important work to be done.

In about six months I left the university without completing my dissertation or taking my final exams. I went to work for Campus Crusade in the headquarters office of EXPLO '72 in Dallas. EXPLO was one of those gigantic evangelical conferences that's supposed to bring the world, or the solar system, to Christ overnight. I believed in it and worked hard for it, though I had trouble getting along in the EXPLO headquarters atmosphere.

The whole thing provided for my Christian experience what boot camp provides for a marine. After working with Campus Crusade I would never again be frustrated by the way the regular people did things. And regular people they were; I was the only Jew in the vast headquarters complex, and there was one black (no Italians). I had to get used to endless rules and regulations, tight discipline, inexplicable dress codes and personal mannerisms, tense group prayers, "infallible superiors" (or so they told me the Bible said) and getting up too early. On the other hand I learned to completely trust the Lord. We prayed—oh, how we prayed! It was *very* hard to put that 100,000-member conference together. I never doubted that the Lord was with us as the thing worked out.

I still had my "us and them" concept of the folks around me, but it was more like "*me* and them" since there was only one of *me*. The Campus Crusade outreach extended only to the regular people and so I began to miss the company of Jews. We never witnessed to Jews, never talked to Jews; we only rented from Jews.

But then an interesting chance to meet with some Jews came my way in the preparations for the conference. We had to find housing for the prodigious numbers of young people who would descend on us during the big week and we had asked various church groups to volunteer space as they could. One of the groups that responded was *Beth Sar Shalom* ("House of the Prince of Peace"), the Dallas branch of the American Board of Missions to the Jews. We normally sent a headquarters member out to see such groups and make the arrangements for the housing, and I was the logical choice for that one, just as Chuck, our house black, went to the blacks.

Well, once I saw Beth Sar Shalom I went back for

services every Friday night, and I still go to this day. The Head Missionary, Dr. Tom McCall, told me Jesus is Jewish and stressed for me the very vital aspects of the mission to my people. I was intrigued.

Tom and I conceived a book together concerning prophecy, and especially the rebuilding of the Temple in Jerusalem. We started working on it just before EXPLO exploded and we sent the manuscript to Moody Press, with the title *Satan in the Sanctuary*. I hoped the publisher would like the book because I was out of work once the conference passed by. Campus Crusade packed up and left and I remained at my typewriter, determined to write for the Lord.

I made my sincerest prayers that summer after EX-PLO. I was still a new enough believer to take the Scriptures at face value; if God said He would feed me like He fed the birds and clothe me like He clothed the lilies of the field, I believed Him. I didn't seek other work; I just waited on God.

I suppose I'll never have that pure a faith again. I've become an experienced Christian now. Back then I was desperate and had to trust God for everything. Now I automatically help Him manage my affairs, which is like helping a surgeon take out your own appendix.

Anyway, I'm still out of work, in effect. Despite my efforts to mastermind my life, the King has made a busy ministry for me. *Satan in the Sanctuary* was accepted and sold a jillion copies. It was re-released by Bantam Books, translated into German, Spanish, Finnish and I don't know what else, and it continues to sell very well. I haven't gotten rich, by any means, but my early books all did well enough to carry me along without my ever having to get up too early again.

I married Yvonne the year after EXPLO. I had managed to talk the EXPLO people into accepting her in Dallas to work at headquarters. I think they relented because they thought, "If we get that screwball's girlfriend down here maybe he'll shape up." They hired Yvonne and things were "really neat," in their parlance.

Yvonne and I now minister together in various ways. I have a talk show, a steady bookwriting ministry, a lot of speaking engagements, films, tapes, a Bible-teaching ministry—emphasizing the Old Testament and the mission to the Jews—and lots of travel and lots of fun. I've been to Israel four times in four years.

I have obviously been put to work in just the way God promised to put the Jews to work if only we would disciple them. In six years the Lord has used me to reach literally millions of people with the gospel. Folks get saved right and left, particularly Jews, and, all things considered, I like life with the King very much. I'm extremely busy being a blessing to people, as God works things out with me. (And believe me, I never was a blessing to anybody before I met God.) God is using me as a Jew, as an evangelist, as a communicator, as a missionary, as a counselor, and in myriad other ways that utterly confuse me. None of my unbelieving friends would have predicted anything even vaguely like this in my life. I was not voted "Most Likely to Succeed" by those regular people who prepared our high school yearbook, and the Italians in my old poolroom just wouldn't know me now.

Obviously the difference has been the influence of the Messiah in my life, and any Jew will respond the same way—and be used in much the same way—when he is saved.

Look at it this way. If you witnessed to just one Jew like Yvonne did, and then that Jew wrote books that sold a million copies, and made films, and talked to 100,000 people per week on the radio, and so forth, don't you think the Lord would be pleased with your ministry?

Don't you think it's worth a try?

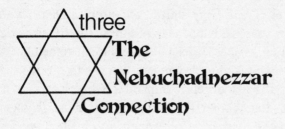

three
The
Nebuchadnezzar
Connection

Okay, that's enough background and preparation. Now we can talk about how to really do it.

Now that you understand where the Jew is coming from, and his natural right to the gospel of Jesus Christ, let's move on to just how we get the Jew and his Messiah together.

I have a certain formula I've come by that seems to put things in order where the Jew is concerned. To witness to the Jew (or anyone else, really) you need to first have fellowship with him. Then you need to take him to the Bible, his own book. And finally you should take him to church; by that I mean a church where the Lord is honored and the Bible taught. (The Jew won't be impressed with a liberal church; his synagogue is much better than that.)

Rev. Gene Getz started a church in Dallas with a name that just happens to put these three factors right in their proper order, and if you can remember the name of his church you can witness to the Jews. He calls the place Fellowship Bible Church.

In this chapter I'm going to talk about *fellowship* with the Jew. The following two chapters will deal respectively with opening the *Bible* for the Jew and taking him to *church*.

Fellowship with Jews presents some special problems because the regular people don't mix with the Jews much. And you know, I think there's a very special theological reason for this. While the Jews have managed to survive any number of Gentile dictatorships and have come down to us as modern, educated people, somehow the idea of oppressing Jews has never died a natural death. Somehow the Jews are never anybody's best friends.

Why does everybody seem to go after the Jews?

The Devil Makes You Do It

Satan could never say, "Some of my best friends are Jewish." He hates the Jews, as we noted briefly earlier. He has good reason. The Jews, simply existing, are the best visible proof of God in the world. The mere presence of the Jews makes many thinking unbelievers give the Bible some credence and God's plan some notice.

Look at it this way. There was once a time when the Jews were one of a hundred wandering, marauding tribes of the Sinai desert. They cast about, here and there, fighting battles, hauling their cumbersome Tabernacle, keeping what must have appeared to the nomads around them as some of the weirdest religious rites in all creation.

When they announced to sundry foes that they were in fact the chosen people, the sundry foes probably said, "Yeah, so are we." Everybody tends to think his own people are the chosen people, and all warriors have God on their side. (The Nazi SS corps, who staffed the concentration camps, wore on their belt buckles the legend *Gott Mit Uns*—"God is with us.")

As time went on, the idea of the Hebrew people being somebody special must have begun to catch on. Chroniclers of the time must have noticed that they did not perish or disband in the wilderness, as had so many other nameless bands of sojourners. They did not change their Law. They did occupy what they referred to as their "Promised Land." They did, under nearly hopeless odds—considering the strength of their enemies, the hardships of the times in general and the constant battleground of the Middle East— form a nation in Israel. They did manage to prosper.

Probably some commentator of 3,000 years ago wrote grudgingly, "You've got to hand it to those Jews. Nobody likes them, but they win their battles and they pay their bills." Probably the attitude of the neighbors toward the Jews didn't vary much from what it is today; a willingness to give credit where it's due but no love lost.

The vitality of the Jewish nation under the mighty

sovereigns David and Solomon must have deeply impressed the ancient world. Jewish travelers took biblical ideas over the seas, so that now we find traces of monotheism and Creator-belief even in the Eastern cultures. Jonah went to Nineveh to enlighten the pagans there about God and the Scriptures indicate that they believed him.

Somewhere in those times Satan must have developed a deep respect for the powers of the chosen people. We can almost see him conceding to God that the Almighty had made an interesting and challenging move in their cosmic chess game. Those infernal Jews were starting to get under the skin of God's adversary. The idea of a people chosen especially to serve God and bless the nations of the world was taking hold.

We can surmise this enmity between the devil and the Jews by what started happening to the Jews. Somehow, despite the overwhelming success of their religious system, they began to drift away from their one-of-a-kind law and become interested in the pagan ways of the people around them. This was specifically forbidden in the Law; God had said time and again, "I am a jealous God," and "Do not even inquire as to how they worship their gods." Paganism of every form was manifestly forbidden for the chosen people.

But Solomon in all his glory, a wealthy and enormously powerful monarch, dallied with foreign wives and concubines until he fell into their religious ways. The king brought to the nation a curiosity about worldly matters that continues among the Jews to this day, to the extreme detriment of their relationship with God.

Things really went to pieces after Solomon. Israel became divided into two kingdoms, weakening the defensive structure of the nation in the always precarious power struggle of the Middle East. Paganism actually became the way of worship of a long line of Judean and Israeli kings, so that we find Manasseh building altars to Baal right in the Temple of God in Jerusalem, and Jeroboam burning foreign incense in an illegally franchised local temple at Bethel (2 Kings 21:3,4; 1 Kings 12:28,29).

Godly kings came along—Hezekiah, Josiah (the latter, in God's opinion, was the best king Israel ever had, 2 Kings 23:25)—but nothing could forestall the judgment of the infuriated Jehovah upon Israel (see 2 Kings 21:11-15). They had responded to the call of Satan and they were going to have to pay the price. They had not harkened to the steady warnings of Isaiah, Jeremiah and a host of other prophets who sounded the alarm on behalf of the patient God of Israel over the centuries; they had not changed their ways in Judah even after the loss of the ten tribes of the north. They were still deeply immersed in the devil's business when God sent "Nebuchadnezzar, the king of Babylon, My servant."

Nebuchadnezzar, who threw down the mighty Temple and carried off 10,000 captives, began a 2,500-year reign of persecution against the Jews just *because* they were Jews. Pharaoh oppressed the chosen people seemingly for the value of their labor; the captains and the kings who fought the Israelites in the wilderness and on the borders of Israel through the ages fought fair and square, trying to seize property as all nations still do.

But Nebuchadnezzar might be called the first anti-Semite.

He was like the devil incarnate. He hated Jewish things, Jewish Law and Jewish people. He did far more than necessary to overpower a nation; he tried to find that elusive "final solution to the Jewish problem." He was one of Satan's key men.

The Jews somehow recovered from this seemingly mortal blow and survived to reoccupy Israel, but only at the pleasure of foreign powers from that time (c. 516 B.C.) until A.D. 1948!

The new kind of persecution, anti-Semitism, was continued through Antiochus Epiphanes who sacrificed a pig on the new Temple altar in Jerusalem (167 B.C.); Titus of Rome, who slaughtered the Jews more efficiently than even Hitler (1.1 million in 5 months in A.D. 70); the Moslems, who chose the site of the ancient Temples to place their Dome of the Rock, still standing very much in the way of God's future plans in Jerusalem; the Crusaders; the Inquisitors; the pagan churches of Rome and the East; the supposedly enlightened Renaissance societies of Europe, who found the Jews somehow not up to the standards of their cultures; and more lately, Stalin, Hitler and the whole Arab world.

We should notice two characteristics of anti-Semitism that are different from the normal everyday op-

43

pression of people that is the way of the world. First, the Jews are detested for no good reason. They haven't really done anything. Second, the anti-Semites, characteristic of those who work arduously for the devil, have marvelous success out of all proportion to the oppression of any people but Jews. The personalities mentioned above—Nebuchadnezzar through Hitler and the Arabs—were always remarkably successful in beating up on the Jews. Hitler's killing of six million stands alone in the history of genocide; no people anywhere, at any time, under any conqueror, have taken anything like that loss. That loss would have been sufficient to totally wipe out any one of a hundred modern or ancient nations. Six million gone in a few years beggars the casualty figures of any war, any oppression, any attempt at wholesale slaughter in the entire story of mankind.

That's the way of the devil. It has to be.

Those who hate the Jews are in league with the devil, it stands to reason.

Look at the success of the modern anti-Semites. The world today seems to hate Israel, as though the existence of that tiny nation makes a big difference in the mighty comings and goings of the great and small powers. A handful of terrorists has incredibly managed to stand the whole world on its ear and persuade people everywhere that the Jews are up to no good again. "Israel must die" is the philosophy of the wealthy and comfortable Arabs, who seem to make the Jews their personal vendetta.

This anti-Semite attitude must be explained supernaturally. Who but the devil could manage to get little Israel on the daily agenda of the United Nations? Who but God's clever adversary could promote the appearance of a common hit-man like PLO terrorist Yasir Arafat before the Security Council of that body, as though he were some sort of statesman?

The anti-Semitism goes on and on, virtually without a stop, since those ancient biblical days when Satan began to appreciate the Jews for what they were and took steps to do something about them.

"I Will Never Forsake Them"

And so we ought to love the Jews as the Lord did.

Fellowship is the first step. Some of your best friends really *ought* to be Jews.

God said time and again concerning His people, even at some of their most irreverent moments, "I will never forsake them!" (see Deut. 4:31; Jer. 31:37, et. al.). Obviously we must have the same attitude if we're to walk with God. He called the Jews, "The apple of My eye."

Loving those whom God loves—at least having fellowship with them—shouldn't be all that difficult. This is not a book on personalities and how to cultivate them, and I'm not a psychologist. But from my own experience I can give a hint or two as to how to cultivate your Jewish neighbor so that he truly becomes one of your best friends.

Keep in mind, if fellowship with Jews presents a difficult challenge for you, then it is an important and godly responsibility. If the Jew is at war with the

45

devil, what he needs is the presence of the Messiah. You have Him. Share Him. Bring Him into the company of the Jew. You will see the Jewish person react to all that is godly within you.

And that's the first piece of counsel I would give on fellowship with the Jew—show him your godliness. Jews are very sensitive to atmospheres. They pick up on subtle things. They will see that your faith is sincere and your motives godly, assuming those things are true of you. (They will quickly discover that you're a phony, if you're a phony. They're good at that. They've had to be.)

Now don't talk in terms of "the blood," "the Saviour" (putting the stress on that 'u'—Sav-*yoor*—so you're speaking true King James), "the Trinity," "the Spirit," and all the rest that the Jew would obviously fail to identify with. You wouldn't use algebra terms in third grade arithmetic; wait until a man is ready to take on the New Testament before you overwhelm him with technical terms and your special knowledge of spiritual things.

You are the most important item in this list. You have been sent to the world—the Jew first—with the message of the gospel. "Be . . . wise as serpents, harmless as doves," the Master counseled (Matt. 10:16).

I remember hearing the Campus Crusade Bible teacher assure us at the office one morning, "We are saved through the blood." I didn't know what it meant at that time, though I had been saved for several months. I remember thinking to myself, "How are we 'saved *through the blood'*? How do we get *through the blood*? Do we swim? Take a boat?"

Spiritual things, Paul points out, are foolishness to the natural man. When witnessing to natural men, speak in their terms. The prime difference between you and an unsaved Jew is that you know his Messiah has already come and he doesn't. Start there, and gently make your point. Jesus didn't think of Nicodemus as stupid; He lovingly outlined the spiritual life for him, and the process of salvation. He gave a complete account, but in keeping with Nicodemus' own knowledge.

Sometimes you just can't get to the gospel when talking to the Jew. Sometimes your Jewish friend won't stand still for that. Well and good. Your spiritual heart will still be apparent to him on any topic. But you do have to get close enough to let him see your heart. He'll sooner or later want to know what makes that spiritual heart tick.

Secondly, do talk about common topics with the Jew. He is not vitally interested in your church, unless he feels your church is going to murder the Jews next Good Friday. My father was deathly afraid of the local Eastern Orthodox and Catholic churches. When he was a boy in Latvia the local "Christians" killed the Jews on Good Fridays as part of their ministry for the Jewish Messiah.

Probably the Jew has looked over your church in passing, and under the circumstances doesn't fear it. I'm going to tell you later on how to take the Jew to church, but for openers you should talk about something else.

Common topics with the Jew are (to mention only a few obvious ones) Israel, the human condition, God, prayer, intellectual things, the American society, the Bible, etc. The Christian and the Jew are both interested in those things, and a host of others. The Jew, being an earthman, is surprisingly like everyone else despite what you may have been told.

In talking about Israel, probably the most important common topic, be sure to have your head straight on the Jew's special love and special right to this land. We have reviewed the covenant about the Jew and Israel; a great place to start is in the recognition of the godly right of the Jewish people to their land.

But prophecy about Israel is more removed from the Jewish person's thinking. He is not aware, and his rabbi is not aware, of what the prophets have said concerning the land. Don't begin, "How do you do, Mr. Ginsburg. Did you know the Russians are going to invade Israel?"

Thirdly, assuming that you have managed to strike up a working relationship with the Jew, know this: it will take a lot of listening on your part to relate to him. The Jews simply love to talk and they have a lot to say. One problem the Jews have with the Gentiles is simply that the Gentiles "don't relate." I have heard many a Jew say, "How can you get to know them? They have too many secrets." What's really being said here is that the Gentile doesn't wear his heart on his sleeve. He's more reserved. The difference in character isn't really Jewish-Gentile. Actually, the Jews are Mediterraneans by background, and

like the Italians, Greeks, Egyptians and so forth, they like to chatter. Most American Gentiles come out of northern stock and have more modest personalities.

Let the Jewish person talk. You'll be well entertained and informed, in most cases, and your Jewish friend will feel more comfortable.

The Jews are social people. They like the give and take of life, and they like it very verbal. Go into a Jewish delicatessen late some Friday night and just listen. The place will be alive with conversation, laughter and good cheer. That's just the way they prefer things and the way they feel best. You don't have to fake a whole new personality—just listen, and react when you talk with a Jew.

Next, you might just try going to a synagogue. You won't catch a strange disease and they won't try to convert you. Most any synagogue is open to all comers, though they won't grab your hand and grin like a bunch of church deacons. You would have a very interesting time going to synagogues of the three branches of Judaism—orthodox, conservative and reform. You will see that the orthodox really mean it when they worship and the reform are somewhere close to that dead church with the big steeple in the rich part of your town. The conservatives vary in between.

My friend Dr. Tom McCall attended a very orthodox storefront synagogue in Los Angeles for some two years. They knew he was a goy, of course, but they accepted him after awhile and good fellowship was the result. Naturally Tom got a witness in, and naturally nobody fell to their knees when he did, but he had a wonderful time and he learned a great deal. And somebody he talked to about the Messiah there may well remember the conversation when the chips are down. I know of cases where a Jew on his death-bed has asked to see once again a missionary who talked to him years and years before. And those cases result in salvations. See my book, *Jesus the Jew's Jew* (Creation House), for some overwhelmingly beautiful and emotional frontline stories of such conversions.

You might like to see the way the Jewish feasts (Lev. 23) are now observed in the synagogues, and you might have your chance to explain what you know about them in Christ, if you have that knowledge. You might just have the chance to point out that the Messiah certainly observed those feasts and was in every way an exemplary Jew.

And finally a last suggestion that pervades all the others: Remember that the Jew can be a very lonely person inside. He can be very afraid of the world at large and very downtrodden just because he is Jewish. This inner insecurity is usually covered over by a surface bravado and a noisy confidence, but I know Jews who fully expect another holocaust and have bad dreams about it all the time. It serves no good purpose to try to talk them out of that (indeed, as prophecy progresses and the Antichrist arrives those bad dreams will become real life). Instead, utilize your discernment to appreciate your friend's hard lot, tragic background and constant struggle with the principalities and powers. The mind of Christ is sufficient to be compassionate to the Jews. May we just use it when the occasion calls.

Now I certainly don't mean to put anyone off by creating a special list of behaviors appropriate to the company of Jews. As I have said above, they are not all *that* special. Actually a little bit of experience with some Jewish people will be worth ten books like this (though I doubt if there *are* ten books about witnessing to the Jews). You will see that a normal amount of sensitivity to the other person will make the grade among the Jews. I could go on and on with special suggestions, but I'd rather you just approach a Jewish acquaintance and get started.

But please, don't just put this book down and forget about it. Do your job. Be ready to answer the Lord about His people.

Let my people go ... to heaven.

four
Give Him the Word

The Jews don't read the Bible anymore, and that's all there is to that.

If you think it's frustrating to get the folks in church to read the Bible, you ought to try to get the Jews to read it.

The Bible is our second element in our FELLOW-SHIP, BIBLE, CHURCH formula of witnessing. You can't witness to anyone successfully without it, and especially not to the Jews.

The People of the Book

The Jews are "the people of the Book," in the sense that they composed the Bible and gave it to the world. There is a beautiful shrine in Israel displaying the

Dead Sea scrolls. It's called "The Shrine of the Book." The Jews take for granted that the Bible is a Jewish artifact, utilized extensively by Jews. Jews are supposed to be Bible experts.

There's no truth to that at all, however. I don't personally know a single Jew who ever really studies the Bible, and I can't think of one out of my past either. True enough, we memorized some psalms in Sunday School, and we reviewed the stories of the patriarchs and prophets of our people. But that sort of exercise is to Bible study what saying the Pledge of Allegiance is to the study of the Constitution.

I emphasize this point because many Christian people (who really aren't such Bible experts either) think that the Jews are way ahead of the church in Bible study. They are intimidated by the idea that Jews are "walking Old Testaments," completely conversant in the Torah and steeped in the prophets. True enough, there are Jews here and there who know some Bible, and in Israel there are some well-studied Bible scholars. But does it stand to reason that people who cannot find the Messiah really know the Scriptures? When I come across people who have never heard of the tribulation period, the Kingdom (not to mention the King), the Rapture and a host of other biblical issues referred to constantly throughout the Bible, I assume that they do not study that book, whether they be Jews or Hottentots. When people make a summary decision about Jesus Christ—He was a "great philosopher," a "benevolent moral teacher" or some other such patronizing mumbo-

jumbo—I cannot call them Bible experts, even if their ancestors did write the Book.

The truth of the matter is, the biblical commentaries—the Talmud and so forth—take precedence over the Bible among the rabbis, and the lay Jewish person has read neither the Scriptures *nor* the commentaries. The average Jew hasn't the vaguest idea of where Jewish law and tradition came from, nor how to separate the two. He doesn't know the Bible and he doesn't know the traditional laws, and that's the long and short of it.

Now, starting from that point, we can talk intelligently about how to help the Jew remedy that situation.

The religion of the Jewish people today is divided into three categories, which really express three levels of the same religion. There are the orthodox, the conservative and the reform.

The *orthodox* Jews are the "most religious" in the sense of doing the most attendance at synagogues and the most law keeping. They conduct lengthy and very solemn services primarily in Hebrew. The *conservatives* do a little less of the law-keeping and synagogue attendance, preferring to keep up with the times by continually updating Judaism. They utilize much more English in the service, keep the feasts in a perfunctory way and generally practice a middle-of-the-road Judaism, not so demanding as the orthodox or so liberal as the reform. The *reform* Jews purvey a "Jewish culture" sort of religion, totally divorced from the Scriptures. They normally discuss social issues and they are, in my estimation, utterly secular.

It might serve the Christian reader better to just compare the three branches of Judaism to three categories into which we generally assign professing Christian churches. So, the orthodox synagogue might well be compared to the highly conservative Christian denominations—Nazarene, perhaps, or Mennonite—in the sense of strict adherence to a code and the best possible perfection of the saints. The conservative Jews are more like the large denominations who still opt for the Scriptures—Southern Baptists, maybe, or the various groups that go by the nomenclature "Bible Church." The reform Jews are like the big liberal denominations who have put the Bible away and are off into their own modernized thing.

It might help you to know which sort of Jewish person you are dealing with in terms of his level of commitment to Judaism when you approach him with the Bible. Generally, those who witness to Jews reach the conclusion that the *more* committed to orthodoxy the particular Jewish person is, the more likely he will come to the Messiah. A reform Jew is rather like a liberal "Christian"—you get the feeling you're beating your head against a wall when you witness. But the orthodox Jew believes in God and takes spiritual matters more seriously.

But when all is said and done, most any Jew will have an underlying respect for his own holy writ. When you demonstrate the Messiah in the Old Testament, you go a long way toward winning the Jew.

The Messiah in the Old Testament

The Messiah appears much earlier in the Bible than most readers appreciate. In Genesis 3:15, God says:

> *And I will put enmity between thee and the woman, and between thy seed and her seed; it shall bruise thy head, and thou shalt bruise his heel.*

Rabbis and Christian scholars alike have traditionally agreed that this passage refers to the Messiah. God is, of course, speaking to the serpent in the garden, who treacherously tempted Eve. He is saying that some future "seed" of a woman will battle Satan ("bruise thy head"). This promised seed will deal Satan a mortal blow while sustaining only a minor injury Himself.

The idea of a woman having the seed is the cryptic part. In normal conception the seed comes from the man. Christian scholars interpret this verse as a subtle reference to the virgin birth—apparently, the Satan destroyer comes forth from a woman alone.

In any case, Genesis 3:15 seems to be the first reference of a long line of ever more definite identifications of the Messiah throughout the Torah. The Pentateuch, or Jewish Torah, can be read as a kind of detective story, where we narrow down step-by-step the identity of the one who fulfills the seed promise.

With the tragic murder of Abel, Adam and Eve might have thought that the seed was destroyed. He was, after all, their more faithful son. However, the

Lord gave Seth to our first parents as a replacement for Abel, and the seed continued through his line to his illustrious descendant, Noah.

"Noah found grace in the eyes of the Lord" and was spared, with his three sons and their wives, from the Flood. The seed promise proceeds to Noah's son, Shem (Gen. 9:26). Shem means "the Name," and is used synonymously with the Lord's Name.

As the Pentateuch record continues to unfold, we see most clearly and intensely that the seed passes to Shem's descendant, Abraham. Messianic prophecy is most explicit in connection with this called-out one:

And in thy seed shall all the nations of the earth be blessed; because thou hast obeyed my voice (Gen. 22:18).

In this part of the Abrahamic covenant we can see its ultimate meaning: Abraham's descendants would bless the world in various ways, but none more emphatically than in the provision of the Messiah Himself (Matt. 1:1).

Of Abraham's two sons, Ishmael and Isaac, God specifically chooses Isaac as the continuation of the promise. Abraham actually appeals on behalf of Ishmael ("O that Ishmael might live before thee"), but God states that His covenant will proceed through Isaac and his line. God says that He will properly honor Ishmael as part of Abraham's seed, but in Isaac his seed "shall be called" (see Gen. 17:18-21).

It is easier with hindsight and the genealogies of the

gospels for us to realize the exact progress of the seed from generation to generation. It might not have been so obvious to Abraham, but the faithful one proceeded according to God's wishes.

Isaac had two sons, Jacob and Esau. Again, God had to make a choice and He elected to continue the seed promise through Jacob (Gen. 28:13,14).

The vast elimination contest continued through the twelve sons of Jacob, with the Lord choosing Judah:

> *The sceptre shall not depart from Judah*
> *... and unto him shall the gathering of the*
> *people be* (Gen. 49:10).

The sceptre, the symbol of royalty, brings in the fact that the Messiah would indeed be King. It is further enhanced in the book of Numbers by a mighty prophecy out of the heathen prophet, Baal:

> *I shall see him, but not now: I shall be-*
> *hold him, but not nigh: there shall come a*
> *Star out of Jacob, and a Sceptre shall rise*
> *out of Israel, and shall smite the corners of*
> *Moab, and destroy all the children of Sheth.*
> *And Edom shall be a possession, Seir also*
> *shall be a possession for his enemies; and*
> *Israel shall do valiantly* (Num. 24:17,18).

The royal power of the coming Messiah is strongly stated in this prophecy in the "Star" and "Sceptre." Baal spoke accurately on this occasion.

The final Messianic promise in the Torah is found in a declaration by God to Moses:

> *I will raise them up a Prophet from among their brethren, like unto thee, and will put my words in his mouth; and he shall speak unto them all that I shall command him. And it shall come to pass, that whosoever will not hearken unto my words which he shall speak in my name, I will require it of him* (Deut. 18:18,19).

This part of the promise identifies the coming Messiah as the prophet. So we have been able to see Him as the enemy of Satan, the coming King, and as a prophet like Moses (who delivered his people out of bondage).

We should appreciate that all the parts of the seed promise which I have recorded here come out of the Jewish Torah. There is hardly a Jew anywhere who cannot muster some respect for the Holy Torah. When it is brought forth in the synagogues, all in the congregation must stand and, as the Torah passes them in the aisle, they must kiss the Torah. (In the orthodox and conservative synagogues, they touch the end of their prayer shawl to the Torah and then to their lips.) This profound respect for the law is generally not found in the reform congregations, I should say, but their members do reverence the Torah as, at least, great Jewish literature.

Obviously, the seed promise argument is potent,

coming as it does out of the Torah. Coupled with the prophecies about the Messiah given in the prophets, it is enough to give an open-minded Jewish person quite a bit of thought.

The Messiah in Prophecy

The birth of the Messiah, His mission and death and His resurrection, are all made very clear in the rest of the Old Testament. It becomes obvious as we proceed that we could be referring to no other individual than Jesus Christ as the details come forth. Up to this point, we have only vaguely identified the Messiah by His lineage and certain characteristics of His power. God revealed Him to be of royal blood out of Judah, and a great prophet. But as we go on, we will see definitive details in prophecy that pertain only to Jesus Christ.

Beginning with the Messiah's birth, the prophets Isaiah and Micah contribute precise details:

> *Therefore the Lord himself shall give you a sign; Behold, a virgin shall conceive, and bear a son, and shall call his name Immanuel* (Isa. 7:14).

> *But thou, Bethlehem Ephratah, though thou be little among the thousands of Judah, yet out of thee shall he come forth unto me that is to be ruler in Israel; whose goings forth have been from of old, from everlasting* (Mic. 5:2).

Thus, the Messiah is indeed born of a virgin, as Genesis 3:15 suggested cryptically. And furthermore He is to be born in Bethlehem, where King David was born. We have thus narrowed the search down to one personality, if these prophecies are to be believed. Occasionally, one may hear some medical rumors of a virgin birth, but God also specified the very town, and it is a small town.

Isaiah went further, proclaiming in magnificent terms the enormity of the birth of this particular Child of Israel:

> *For unto us a child is born, unto us a son is given: and the government shall be upon his shoulder: and his name shall be called Wonderful, Counsellor, The mighty God, The everlasting Father, The Prince of Peace. Of the increase of his government and peace there shall be no end, upon the throne of David, and upon his kingdom, to order it, and to establish it with judgment and with justice from henceforth even for ever. The zeal of the Lord of hosts will perform this* (Isa. 9:6,7).

As to the mission of the Messiah and His death, there is no better reference than the entire chapter of Isaiah 53. Throughout the prophets, one finds innumerable references to the Messiah's sacrifice, the blood which grants us salvation, and the ultimate purpose of this magnificent act of God. But Isaiah becomes extremely detailed on the precise circumstances of the Messiah's sacrifice. The entire fifty-third chapter of Isaiah should be read, beginning with Isaiah 52:13, and understood by every Christian. It is a powerful witness not only to the Jews, but to any human being conscious of his sins. Isaiah pictures perfectly the intercessory act of Jesus Christ on the cross. And it might be pointed out that the Dead Sea scrolls unquestionably establish the date of Isaiah's prophecy at several centuries before Christ:

> *For he shall grow up before him as a tender plant, and as a root out of a dry ground: he hath no form nor comeliness; and when we shall see him, there is no beauty that we should desire him. He is despised and rejected of men; a man of sorrows, and acquainted with grief: and we hid as it were our faces from him; he was despised, and we esteemed him not.*
>
> *Surely he hath borne our griefs, and carried our sorrows: yet we did esteem him stricken, smitten of God, and afflicted. But he was wounded for our transgressions, he was bruised for our iniquities: the chastisement of our peace was upon him; and with his stripes we are healed. All we like sheep have gone astray; we have turned every one to his own way; and the Lord hath laid on him the iniquity of us all (Isa. 53:2-6).*

The very details of the Messiah's trial and death are given by the great prophet:

He was oppressed, and he was afflicted, yet he opened not his mouth: he is brought as a lamb to the slaughter, and as a sheep before her shearers is dumb, so he openeth not his mouth. He was taken from prison and from judgment: and who shall declare his generation? For he was cut off out of the land of the living: for the transgression of my people was he stricken (Isa. 53:7,8).

The highly evocative and emotional chapter ends with the simple statement:

And he bare the sins of many, and made intercession for the transgressors (v. 12).

Many Jewish people have come to realize the mission of Jesus Christ through reading this one biblical chapter. It presents so beautifully not only the facts of the atoning death of the Messiah, but also the logic of it. Since God asked for the blood for remission of sins (Lev. 17:11), and the Israelites dutifully conducted their animal sacrifices over the millennia, then the Lamb of God obviously follows. God, in effect, made the last sacrifice—the one that set His people free.

Of course, if the Old Testament had only reported the death of Christ and not His resurrection, the argument would be weak. How should we be saved by one who could simply be eliminated from the human race? But the resurrection is also clear in the Old Testament. Peter skillfully applied King David's Psalm 16 on the occasion of the coming of the Holy Spirit at Pentecost. He was confronted with a crowd of thousands of Jewish people celebrating their harvest feast (Lev. 23:15,16), when the Spirit descended on them. On that occasion, he delivered the five-minute sermon that saved 3,000 Jewish people.

The heart of Peter's reasoning about the resurrection of Christ was David's writing, well known by Peter's audience (Acts 2:25-28). Peter referred to David's statement—

> *For thou wilt not leave my soul in hell; neither wilt thou suffer thine Holy One to see corruption* (Ps. 16:10)

—in showing that Christ was risen. We might take a cue from the great fisherman and also quote this powerful psalm.

Sometimes the Jewish people object to the resurrection on the grounds that the Jewish religion does not hold to life after death at all. However, the prophet Daniel is most clear on this issue:

> *And many of them that sleep in the dust of the earth shall awake, some to everlasting life, and some to shame and everlasting contempt. And they that be wise shall shine as the brightness of the firmament; and they*

that turn many to righteousness as the stars
for ever and ever (Dan. 12:2,3).

The Messiah rose from the dead and, moreover, according to the New Testament those believing in Him will also be resurrected:

> *For as in Adam all die, even so in Christ*
> *shall all be made alive. But every man in his*
> *own order: Christ the firstfruits; afterward*
> *they that are Christ's at his coming* (1 Cor.
> 15:22,23).

After this much biblical proof concerning the promises of the Messiah and His actual birth, His mission and His death, and finally His resurrection, the open-minded Jewish person should be impressed. But sometimes there is a recoil, even in the face of what the Scriptures plainly say. This reaction usually takes the form of, "But it's just not Jewish to believe in Jesus Christ."

There is some truth to that, although it is the sin of men and not the plan of God that has made it come out that way. There are many Christian people about who don't understand the Jews, the prophecies in the Bible, the return of the Lord and all of its circumstances, and the ultimate outworkings of all of God's plans. They belong to a Christian club, which just doesn't include Jews—and the Jews very well know it.

However, it is biblically *very* Jewish to become a

follower of Christianity—the New Covenant. The advent of the Lord is the New Covenant, and the New Testament is simply the story of the founding and ultimate triumph of the New Covenant. The Jewish person may be surprised to see the advent of the New Covenant announced plainly by the prophet Jeremiah:

> *Behold, the days come, saith the Lord, that I will make a new covenant with the house of Israel, and with the house of Judah: Not according to the covenant that I made with their fathers in the day that I took them by the hand to bring them out of the land of Egypt; which my covenant they brake, although I was an husband unto them, saith the Lord.*
>
> *But this shall be the covenant that I will make with the house of Israel; After those days, saith the Lord, I will put my law in their inward parts, and write it in their hearts; and will be their God, and they shall be my people. And they shall teach no more every man his neighbour, and every man his brother, saying, Know the Lord: for they shall all know me, from the least of them unto the greatest of them, saith the Lord: for I will forgive their iniquity, and I will remember their sin no more (Jer. 31:31-34).*

That last phrase describes Christianity in the simplest possible terms. Because of the Messiah, our sins are forgiven and forgotten. Because of His death, we live. If it were not Jewish to believe this, then it's hard to say why it is announced by a Jewish prophet; accomplished by the Jew, Jesus Christ, and reiterated for the benefit of the church by the Jewish apostle Paul (see Heb. 8:8-12).

The Bible Tells Him So

Thus, we see the Old Testament is filled with the details of Jesus' ministry and identifies Him plainly. If nothing else will help in showing your Jewish friend that Jesus is his Messiah, you can depend on the fact that the Bible tells him so.

A country preacher once quoted to me the excellent maxim, "The Bible is a lion; you don't have to defend it. Just turn it loose and it will defend itself."

But, of course, the Christian witness must take the trouble to understand these Old Testament references and be able to use them effectively at a moment's notice. The apostles certainly did no less—freely quoting the Jewish Scriptures as the occasion called and reaping great harvests. It might be pointed out that the Messiah Himself utilized the Scriptures most skillfully and effectively, quoting the book of Deuteronomy more than 100 times in His teaching.

In this section, I have given the basics on finding the Messiah in the Old Testament. I want to point out that there is certainly much more to know, and I would like to suggest that the Christian reader, who is serious about witnessing to the Jews contact one of the Jewish missions for further biblical information. There is a fine little book called *The Jewish Bible Approach*, by Manny Brotman, which is available from the Messianic Jewish Movement, International, 7315 Wisconsin Avenue, Washington, D.C. 20014. Further materials, in a contemporary vein, can be gotten from the mission called Jews for Jesus, Box 3558, San Rafael, California 94902. The American Board of Missions to the Jews is the oldest and largest of the Jewish evangelism organizations, and can provide truckloads of excellent biblical materials. If you are in a large city, a local chapter of the mission, complete with Messianic services, is probably within reach. You can take your Jewish friend there, if he'll go. Contact them at 460 Sylvan Avenue, Englewood Cliffs, New Jersey 07632. The author's Bible study tapes are available from Liberation Tapes; Box 6044; Lubbock, Texas 79413.

And as you set out to witness to the seed of Abraham, the Jewish people, bear in mind the most definitive Scripture of them all on this subject, "I will bless them that bless thee."

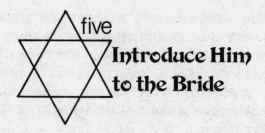

five
Introduce Him to the Bride

First and foremost, make sure that your church is able to show the Jew what you want him to see.

According to God's optimum plan, the Christian church is supposed to make the Jew jealous. Paul discussed this point in his letter to a church that apparently was not witnessing to Jews much, the church at Rome. He wrote first to assure them that the Jew had not somehow fallen out of God's favor (see Rom. 1:16; 10:1; 11:1). "I say then, Have they stumbled that they should fall? God forbid: but rather through their fall salvation is come unto the Gentiles, for to provoke them to jealousy" (Rom. 11:11). Or to paraphrase Paul's meaningful thought: "Is God finished with the Jews? Not by a long shot! On the contrary, the very failure of the Jews to take advantage of the

Kingdom when it was offered has provided for *Gentile salvation*. And Gentile salvation is intended to provoke the Jews back to their Messiah."

God had expressed that very thought long before, back in the early times of the law: "I will move them to jealousy with those which are not a people," the Father declared (Deut. 32:21), indicating that He could well call forth another chosen people out of the masses of the pagan world. He has done that and it is now necessary, for the sake of *Jewish* salvation, for that new chosen people, the church, to make the Jews jealous.

How do you make a Jew jealous? Show him that you have what he needs.

The trouble is, most of the time the church has acted toward the Jew in a way that would hardly make him even respectful of the church, to say nothing of jealous. The Father wants the Jew to *envy* the Christian. Instead, the Jew has tended to almost pity the Christian.

I went to church a couple of times in my college years. I remember entering with some trepidation, thinking I was commiting some vague sin fooling around with pagans, but I was invited by friends who meant well. This was long before anyone seriously witnessed to me; I usually went along with Gentile girlfriends who were trying to "humanize" me.

I remember distinctly my impressions of the Protestant and Catholic churches I attended. I sort of liked the Catholic thing better, probably because it came closer to copying the grandness of my own

73

conservative synagogue, but I was turned off by the ritual around me. The holy water, the confession booths and all the rest were simply too removed from my experience for me to be impressed. Not in my wildest dreams would I get jealous of what was going on there, in any case. The Protestant church seemed dull and dreary—no action, no tone. The people seemed to be making a sort of sacrifice; they were willing to come in and be suffocated with boredom once a week to appease their God, I thought.

Now that, of course, is what you *don't* want to happen when you take your Jewish friend to church. I'm assuming that you have completed steps one and two—you've developed *fellowship* with him and you've opened the *Bible* to him. *Now* the idea is to show him fellowship and Bible *in action.* If your church doesn't really have a rich fellowship that can be sensed by an outsider, and if it doesn't teach the Bible, it's no place for a Jew (or a Gentile).

But, as I have indicated earlier, there are different types of Jews having different types of personalities. You should be able to discern whether your friend will be able to identify with your particular church or with some other kind.

What the Jew needs to get jealous of is sincerity and truth. His own worship is shot through with community standards, cultural preferences, social action and all the rest of the peripheral gibberish of liberals everywhere. He needs to see God being worshiped, not in the Gentile way but in the true way. He has a built-in sense of what is right in worshiping God ("We know what we worship: for salvation is of the Jews," John 4:22) and a subtle recognition of what is sincere and what is not. Remember, he's lived a lot of places and seen a lot of things.

The Special-Event Theory

The special-event theory of bringing a Jew to church says that there has to be some particular reason for him to attend. Perhaps a Jewish person is to be baptized, or a Jewish Christian is to speak. Or perhaps it's one of those "special-evenings-of-hospitality-for-our-Jewish-friends," held once a year whether the church needs it or not.

I don't want to seem unappreciative of church efforts to reach out to the Jew in this way, but let's face it—some Jews will be uncomfortable if they are made to feel that they're only supposed to come when there's a special occasion. If the Christian church is not open to the Jew at all times it's not the Christian church. Something is terribly wrong if those who started the whole thing are not welcome anytime.

But the special-event theory can be very effective, in certain circumstances. It depends on the person, on the church, on the event, and especially on *you*. I rather like people to bring the Jews when I speak in a church because I usually get some chance for a dialogue with them. But admittedly there are some Jews who would rather eat pork and beans than hear me speak. Christians somehow drag them in anyway and we have an uncomfortable situation, to say the least. You must make a well-considered judgment based on the personality of your Jewish friend.

Baptisms are probably not the most acceptable excuse for getting a Jewish person to your church. Although the Jews initiated the concept of purification by water (Exod. 29:4), most of them don't know that they did. In fact, orthodox law has it that once a Jew gets baptized he may not rejoin the synagogue or be buried in a Jewish cemetery. Baptism is where the orthodox draw the line. The baptized Jew is a traitor to them.

So, it's a bit hazardous to say to your Jewish friend, "Mr. Cohen is to be baptized tonight. You just *have* to see this!"

The infamous Jewish Dinner Night has its hazards, too. I rather enjoy these get-togethers, mainly because the churches that undertake them usually buy the best Jewish food from a good deli, but I know the Jews feel a bit awkward about them. Usually the program that goes with the meal is a bit forced. The church has obviously gone out of its way to come up with something of interest to the Jew, and the Jews feel obliged to like it, even in the strange surroundings.

But again, let me qualify. I've seen wonderful evenings spent with Jews and Gentiles in rich fellowship over fine dinners. The Jew feels welcome to return to the church if the evening was sensitively planned, and this is certainly all to the good. Again, it depends on the Jew, on the church, on the evening, etc., etc.

Better by far than the special-event theory of inviting the Jew to church is the spontaneous offer that grows naturally out of the fellowship and Bible interest that have been established. It's really so much better if you are able to say something like, "I like you, and I want you to see my church. It's part of me." If the Jew goes because you go, that's the best way.

And he *will* get jealous if you and your church are doing your jobs. Believe me, I've been to the synagogue and I've been to the church—the church is better. But I'm talking about a church of believers that teaches the Word and honors the Messiah, of course. What the Jew will get jealous of—what he doesn't already have—is the true faith.

If your church has it, take the Jew there.

A Tourist's Guide to Church

Taking a Jew to church—even a fine church—can be like taking someone on a dangerous jungle safari. This is partly because of his preconceptions and partly because of what goes on in the church.

"Forced fellowship" is anathema to the Jew. He's had enough of Gentiles protesting, "But we like you!" The Russians liked Israel in 1948, and they helped vote that nation into the UN. They thought the Jews were going to make some kind of socialistic state over there, with their communal farms and sharing systems. But the Reds don't know Jews very well. The Israelis really *do* share, which makes them different from the Communists, and Jews everywhere are deeply committed to human rights.

The Jews have come out on the short end of too

many false friendships to get into anything but the best. It has to be genuine for the Jew to buy it. So, to begin with, don't tell anyone in your church that you're bringing your friend. Don't set them up to put on a show for the Jew.

You should walk your friend right past those awful hand-pumpers in the doorways. Now I realize the hand-pumpers have the best of intentions. But again, your friend is a tough customer. His first impressions are important. I *still* avoid those deacons and ushers at the church, and I've been going for years. I just have a deep-seated Jewish suspicion of any Gentile who appears to be overly-accepting, as any Jew does.

The other important manifestation of the church turn-off is the one-shot evangelist. This guy is going to personally get your friend saved if it kills them both. Avoid him at all costs. Here you are, having done a great work in developing fellowship with your Jewish friend and getting him to look into the Bible, and up comes the local resident evangelist with his complimentary pass to heaven. That's all you need!

The one-shot evangelist usually thinks he's very subtle, a good listener and a shrewd salesman. He thinks he can fool the Jew into the Kingdom. He puts on the spiritual dog for the Jew.

Bringing a Jew to church and bringing him to salvation are quite different things. We witness to people, such as our witness is; the Lord saves them. Organizations that utilize one-shot evangelism techniques almost never bring Jews to the Lord.

You see, the Jew *fears* salvation. He doesn't understand it as distinct from simple assimilation into the Gentile community—a thing to really be feared. He thinks he will stop being Jewish if he comes to the Messiah.

And let's face it, a trip to the very meeting house of the enemy—the local church—does make the Jew feel as though he's joining up, to some degree. He was raised on that "us and them" conception of humanity, and that idea dies hard.

Look at the fear expressed in the following newspaper article, which ran in the *Louisville Courier Journal*, May 22, 1977:

> *Representatives of Jewish communities in America's urban centers are forming "task forces on missionary activities." The reason: Jews increasingly are prime targets for conversion by America's growing religious cults.*
>
> *According to the American Jewish Committee, such groups as Sun Myung Moon's Unification Church, the Jews for Jesus movement and Hare Krishna people are posing a "growing and serious challenge to Jewish continuity and survival in America."*

That last statement deserves some special attention because it says a lot about the Jewish position toward witnessing in general and Christianity in particular. The American Jewish Committee feels that evangelism of the Jew will actually affect "Jewish continuity and survival in America," and they don't separate evanglism by true Christians (Jews for Jesus) from that done by cultists. They simply don't see the difference between the Messiah's own followers and the odd assortment of latter-days religionists that have come to us according to His prophecies: "Many shall come in my name, saying, I am Christ; and shall deceive many" (Matt. 24:5). The Jew can't tell what a Christian is anymore.

That's our fault.

The responsibility for that confusion lies squarely on the non-witnessing, non-understanding, ever-so-slightly-anti-Semitic Christian church. Far from our making the Jew jealous, we have failed to even gain his recognition. We are the same as these false prophets in his mind.

Now I've been to the churches of the competition. I toured meeting houses of both the Unification Church and the Hare Krishna movement. I can tell you something about them in the spirit of comparing them to the Christian church.

What hits you when you enter either of those cult meeting houses is that the people are "true believers." By golly, the Moonies really worship Rev. Moon and the Hare Krishna's do their thing as though their guru were always looking over each shoulder. When I infiltrated the Moonie headquarters in New York City (which is really just an old hotel now refurbished into a combination fund- and soul-collecting depot) I saw real "faith." They really do believe they're bringing in the Kingdom of God, though their master's theology is simply awful (see my book *The Spirit of Sun Myung Moon*, Harvest House, 1976).

The Hare Krishna folks not only bow down to their guru's throne, which waits resplendently for the promised pilgrimage of some modern-day reincarnation of Krishna, but they also bow down to empty sacred rooms. They constantly murmur incantations, make obeisances to their officers and generally give off the attitude that all the rest of us are religiously very square. They really live their faith. They educate their children in it (and dress them in those outfits) and they eat, drink and sleep Krishna. They chant, they ring cymbals, they sell their incense, they stop people in airports and on the streets—as do the Moonies and the Jews for Jesus—and it would be perfectly fair to say that they are very religious indeed.

Now frankly, their evangelism is better than ours. They put more into it. They're more excited about it and they really work at it—far better than we do in the true church. And when the Jew compares faiths, as he is apt to do in these days of spiritual search in so many directions, he is likely to be quite impressed —especially if that Jew is an intense young person.

I'll tell you what I felt like as a Jew and as a Christian when I confronted those cultists. As a Jew I felt somewhat awed by the very mysticism. Mysticism— that feeling that there is a special way, a transcendental, behind-the-scenes way to God known only unto a few—is sort of Jewish in character. There is a genuine "chosen people" flair to some of these new cults.

More than a few theologians have surmised that the Eastern ideals came from ancient Israel to begin with, and these are very definitely Eastern religions that we are seeing on American streets today. As a Christian I felt spiritually appalled, of course.

In any case, these cults do work powerfully in the Jewish community, for whatever reasons, and they have attracted the attention of the Jewish leadership. Combine their special charisma for the Jew with the church's general lack of concern about the Jew altogether, and you have the reason why more Jewish young people are likely to go off into a cult than into a true church.

Now the American Jewish Committee would quite rightly fear for the survival of American Jewry if every Jewish young person were to be shanghaied by such antibiblical forces. But their fear of the Jews for Jesus is another matter altogether. Jews become more Jewish, in point of fact, when they come to the Jewish Messiah. What could be more simple and rational?

Those Jews who find Jesus as their Messiah tend to go back to the Bible—or go to it for the first time in their lives. They tend to talk with God again. They gain a new understanding of Judaism as the magnificent ideal God made, rather than as some sort of cultural phenomenon. They tend to go all out for God, as we have seen.

So, to recap all that, keep in mind that you are not the only evangelist dispensing the divine light. (As a matter of fact the youthful guru Maharaj Ji provides just that; he assembled tens of thousands of youngsters in the Astrodome in Houston and provided each of them with what he called "The Divine Light.") To the spiritually unaware Jewish person you are merely one of many kinds of evangelists, and your meeting house may actually look pale by comparison. Your church may look very sleepy beside the hyped-up households of Krishna or the computerized nerve centers of the Unification Church.

Be aware, too, that your Jewish friend may have been thoroughly warned about you, as though you were a member of a strange cult out to debilitate Judaism. Realize that the competition is very able because their true leader is the prince of this world.

Your church must offer, in the way of true spiritual grace, what the enemy can offer in the way of fascination and intrigue. Your music, your prayers, your people, must all reflect Almighty God so securely and obviously that all other alternatives can be seen for what they really are. The Jew is sensitive enough to pick up on religious sincerity and true faith.

Just be certain that sincerity and true faith are really there when you take him to your church.

"Pray Without Ceasing"

The Christian church and the Jewish people have one vast and powerful manifestation of faith in common—they both pray. And what's more, they pray to the same God in heaven.

Prayer is real to the Jew. The Jew, unless he's a sworn agnostic, has real respect for prayer. He understands confession of sin, or at least he is aware that

85

confession is the spirit of the all-important high holy day, Yom Kippur (the Day of Atonement). And he does conceive of a listening and reacting God if he's any sort of Jew in his heart.

Of all things that might go on in your church the Jew will likely be most impressed by the prayer. Assuming that your church has a vital prayer ministry, the Jewish person will sense its reality. He may not concede that your prayers will "work" on God, but he'll give you the credit for the faith it takes to pray.

I remember clearly that when Yvonne was witnessing to me it was her prayers that really moved me. One night she prayed right in front of me. "Dear Lord," she began, with her eyes closed and her face composed in that classical picture of sincere entreaty to God. I could not be so coldhearted as to assume that she was merely deluded. I could see that she was talking to Somebody. I could actually feel the presence of that Listener. I came away from her that night with a full realization that God did indeed exist and that He was available. And I was *jealous* of Yvonne's special "in" with Him!

So, if the need comes up in the nature of your relationship with your Jewish friend, offer to pray with him. Or offer to pray *for* him, in his presence. He may decline that offer but there's surely no harm done. In fact, he'll value your concern. And if he agrees we can know that God will be well aware of his presence and what he needs.

If your friend has seen solid Christian prayer in your church he will be that much more likely to appreciate both its informality and its power. He may be surprised, you should know, to see people talking to God in their own words, singly or in groups, and pretty much whenever they want to. The synagogue is infinitely more formal, with prayer only in selected groupings and—in the orthodox synagogue—only by the men. The prayers are formalized to a degree that would stupify a Roman Catholic, and many times the people just listen to them, rather than actually utter them.

I could take a chapter for prayer, of course. But all I will say here is that if Jesus thought prayer was needed to save the Jews, you ought to accept that. How he prayed for His people! And how the apostles prayed for His people! We should surely do no less.

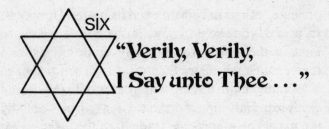

six

"Verily, Verily, I Say unto Thee ..."

Jesus saved the Jewish people by talking to them. The spoken dialogue, the simple conversation about spiritual matters, is certainly the most potent of all witnessing tools. You can have the richest fellowship in the world with a Jewish friend, a very thorough Bible knowledge to share with him and the finest and most spiritual church to take him to, but ultimately his heart will be won through what you *say*.

Jesus did many miracles in the course of His witnessing to the Jewish people, and yet not a great many were saved. He taught the Old Testament Scriptures unerringly, and personally fulfilled many of the prophecies but still left the Jews debating. Some were saved, of course, but the majority were not.

But in His great dialogues, with crowds and with individuals, Jesus seemed to obtain salvations. Confronting the Lord face-to-face, some of the most resistant people were turned to the true life in Christ.

Nicodemus and the Samaritan woman, whom Jesus interviewed in John 3 and John 4, respectively, are excellent examples of individuals won by an expert Christian dialogue. The two were hardly very spiritual when they approached the Lord, and they roughly represent two vast groups of Jews that you will confront today. Nicodemus was biblically oriented and obviously a seeker after a finer spiritual experience. The Samaritan woman was extremely liberal, really only half Jewish, and had a head full of ideas about non-biblical worship.

We'll review the fascinating dialogues the Lord had with these two, and then proceed to contemporary dialogues that might occur when you witness to today's Jewish person.

"Except a Man Be Born Again"

Nicodemus was the sort of Jew that we might refer to today as "open." He was certainly willing to seek out the Teacher and to inquire just how it was that this seemingly ordinary carpenter of Galilee had achieved such an enviable level of spirituality. In Nicodemus' eyes, Jesus was a Jew who had pristine faith, total biblical knowledge, and was near to God Almighty.

Thus, he came forward by night, this orthodox or conservative Jew (in today's terms), respectfully calling Jesus "Rabbi," and referring to Him as one who had surely come from God.

On such on occasion, the Lord did not beat around the bush:

> *Jesus answered and said unto him, Verily, verily, I say unto thee, Except a man be born again, he cannot see the kingdom of God* (John 3:3).

Jesus certainly comes to the point. Perceiving that Nicodemus has every sort of knowledge of God except the ultimate knowledge of salvation by faith, He simply begins at that point. Nicodemus has to be saved—born again.

The scholar answers with a question, a tendency of good debaters everywhere and Jews in particular:

> *Nicodemus saith unto him, How can a man be born when he is old? Can he enter the second time into his mother's womb, and be born?* (John 3:4).

We get the feeling that Nicodemus' question is rhetoric. He doesn't really think a grown man can re-enter his mother's womb to be born again, but he wishes to hear Jesus say more—to perhaps use clear and objective terms, rather than a metaphor to tell him what he wants to know.

We must be aware today that we fall into such metaphors when we try to witness. We find ourselves saying "We are saved through the blood," or simply "Jesus saves," and we are speaking metaphorically. We're not really giving the facts; we're describing something familiar to us but totally alien to our Jewish listener (and to many non-Jewish listeners). We must be ready to follow up with ordinary, worldly terms, as the Lord was:

> *The wind bloweth where it listeth, and thou hearest the sound thereof, but canst not tell whence it cometh, and whither it goeth: so is every one that is born of the Spirit"* (John 3:8).

The Lord said more, of course, and I would encourage you to study the entire chapter to get the force of the whole dialogue. Here, I am trying to pick out the high points. With this explanation the Lord has simply revealed that the Spirit He speaks of is a tangible thing, like the wind. The wind may be used to drive a sailing ship or separate wheat from chaff. But although its force and usefulness may be detected, the wind cannot be seen. So it is with the Holy Spirit, Jesus tells Nicodemus. The force of His enabling ministry is obvious to all believers, but the Spirit Himself is invisible.

Nicodemus again answers with one of those open-ended questions: "Nicodemus answered and said unto him, How can these things be?" (John 3:9).

The Lord now goes into Scriptural proofs from the Old Testament, by way of illustration:

*And as Moses lifted up the serpent in the
wilderness, even so must the Son of man be
lifted up: That whosoever believeth in him
should not perish, but have eternal life. For
God so loved the world, that he gave his only
begotten Son, that whosoever believeth in
him should not perish, but have everlasting
life* (John 3:14-16).

Nicodemus, as an Old Testament scholar, would
have been quite familiar with Moses' serpent in the
desert. The Israelites had been bitten by poisonous
snakes and appealed to Moses for a solution. God
told Moses to place this bronze serpent on a stick and
hold it up before the people. They had only to look
up at the serpent and their wounds were healed (see
Num. 21:6-9). The Lord expertly interprets for
Nicodemus that the Jews still need only to look at sin
(the serpent) lifted up on a stick (nailed to the cross).
And He certifies that He Himself will be "lifted up."

The Lord is illustrating what is known as a "Bible
type"—a symbol in the Old Testament fulfilled in the
New Testament. For a listener of Nicodemus' knowledge, types can be devastating. Likewise, with today's
Jew, such obvious types as the deliverance from
Egypt by the blood of the Lamb, or the concept of
sacrifices yielding redemption as in the ancient Temples, will be very potent. Of course, we are talking
again about a biblical Jew—one who has read and
understood the basic lessons of the Old Testament.

Jesus then decisively illustrates for Nicodemus the

difference between salvation through God's only begotten Son, and the difficulty with the attempt to keep the law:

> *For God sent not his Son into the world to condemn the world; but that the world through him might be saved* (John 3:17).

The Lord points out that the law condemned people, but the Son of God saves them. Nicodemus, definitely a lawkeeper, could appreciate and rejoice at this distinction.

Thus, the Lord Himself chose to speak to Nicodemus in a highly biblical way, with reference to the knowledge of the Old Testament that the ruler already had. In the case of Nicodemus—and in the case of the true seeker among today's Jews—one may freely utilize the Old Testament lessons. The Scriptures given in chapter 5 are appropriate, and additional types and symbols, such as that the Lord used about the serpent, are freely available in many Bible commentaries.

Later in the chapter, in our section on modern dialogues, we can illustrate the effective use of some of these Bible types.

"In Spirit and in Truth"

Now, in the Samaritan woman we see a prideful sort of unbeliever. With all of her sins, she still lays claim to "our father Jacob," and emphasizes her "chosen people" status before the Lord. The Samaritans originally were a mixture of early Northern Israelites and transplanted Assyrian captives. The Samaritan woman could fairly claim Jewish lineage, but her ancestors on both sides had an awful reputation when it came to obeying the will of Jehovah. Still, she is a talkative woman, interested in spiritual matters and apparently quite used to conversation with strange men. She thought nothing of entering into a lengthy dialogue with the unknown traveler from Jerusalem, although for a newly acquainted man and a woman to engage in public conversation was generally frowned upon in Israel at that time.

Jesus again begins His witness with a profound statement of spiritual truth:

> *Jesus answered and said unto her, If thou knewest the gift of God, and who it is that saith to thee, Give me to drink; thou wouldest have asked of him, and he would have given thee living water* (John 4:10).

The woman perceives that the Lord refers to religious matters and asks,

> *Art thou greater than our father Jacob, which gave us the well, and drank thereof himself, and his children, and his cattle?* (John 4:12).

The dialogue progresses until Jesus tells the woman her rather unspiritual past. By this, the Lord is obviously reminding her that she's in some spiritual need. She changes the subject, moving on to theological tangles, which may well represent the diversions that issue from the Jews today:

> *Our fathers worshipped in this mountain; and ye say, that in Jerusalem is the place where men ought to worship* (John 4:20).

The Lord quickly cuts through the woman's reasoning with a powerful statement:

> *But the hour cometh, and now is, when the true worshippers shall worship the Father in spirit and in truth: for the Father seeketh such to worship him. God is a Spirit: and they that worship him must worship him in spirit and in truth* (John 4:23,24).

At that, the Samaritan woman owns up to the fact that she has been awaiting the Messiah, just as many Jews today are awaiting the Messiah:

> *The woman saith unto him, I know that Messias cometh, which is called Christ: when he is come, he will tell us all things* (John 4:25).

Jesus does not let her wait any longer:

> *I that speak unto thee am he* (John 4:26).

The interesting part of the conversion of the Samaritan woman is that her witness immediately bore fruit. She went back into her town testifying about her experience.

> And many of the Samaritans of that city believed on him for the saying of the woman, which testified, He told me all that ever I did. So when the Samaritans were come unto him, they besought him that he would tarry with them: and he abode there two days (John 4:39,40).

The Samaritans then came to hear Jesus in person, and many conversions were made by the Lord's own testimony. This scene certainly demonstrates the power of a seed properly sown. We do not actually learn of the Samaritan woman's conversion, although it seems obvious by the context, but we certainly do see that many people of her town came to the Lord because she made them curious enough to inquire at the source. These latter salvations were accomplished by the testimony of the Lord Himself rather than the woman:

> And many more believed because of his own word; and said unto the woman, Now we believe, not because of thy saying: for we have heard him ourselves, and know that this is indeed the Christ, the Saviour of the world (John 4:41,42).

You may witness to Jew after Jew, seemingly hitting your head against the wall and not seeing any come to the Lord. But please know that Jewish people tend to remember what is said to them and to carry it further. And the saved Jew is a powerful witness. The Lord went so far as to say in this same dialogue that "salvation is of the Jews" (John 4:22). Naturally, this came to pass as the Jewish apostles went forth into the world after the Lord's ascension. How wonderful it would be for the cause of the Lord if we would again disciple the Jews.

The dialogue with the Samaritan woman differs from that with Nicodemus in the fact that she is not nearly so learned nor sincere a seeker. Nevertheless, the Lord, by cutting right through to the truth and dealing with thoroughly scriptural principles, wins her over. He is not so subtle with her as to suggest a cryptic type, like the bronze serpent, because she probably would not appreciate the underlying meaning. But neither does He refrain from telling her who the Messiah is when the opportunity comes.

In general, the interview with the Samaritan woman shows the Lord being very tactful, considerate of her feelings, and still truthful to the Word. With Nicodemus, He spoke in profound spiritual terms, moving directly into the kind of scriptural material that a studied Jew could appreciate. But with the woman, He stayed more on the surface in serving her needs.

The Lord said to His disciples and to us, "You shall do even greater things than these" (see John 14:12).

Let's go on, now, to some hypothetical modern dialogues that you may very well encounter as you witness to today's Jews.

Talking to the Biblical Jew

Let me now recklessly propose some dialogues predicting the reactions of the biblical Jew. Naturally, we can't expect anything like these words to occur, but out of my own experience, I will try to give a composite picture of what usually happens.

In the following dialogue let's call you "Joshua," as a representative of Jesus, and your Jewish friend "Nick," as a representative of Nicodemus. The following conversation might come somewhere close to what you and your friend might say as you discuss the gospel:

Josh: Nick, I realize you have some compunctions in talking about the New Testament. But I am sure you understand that my religion means a great deal to me. I'd like to share it with you.

Nick: Well, my religion means a great deal to me too and I don't need a new one.

Josh: Well, I am not really offering a new one; as a matter of fact, I am offering you the fulfillment of your old one. After all, the Messiah was Jewish and He ministered in Israel. I guess you can appreciate that that makes the Christian faith somewhat Jewish.

Nick: Yes, I can understand that Judaism is the background of Christianity, but it seems to me that my people and yours took two different roads when your Jesus came along.

Josh: Well, Jesus certainly spoke the Old Testament, didn't He? I mean, it was the only Bible of His day and if you look in the gospel you'll find the Torah quoted throughout. He was an orthodox Jew; He kept the Law and He tried to bring the people closer to God.

Nick: I'll grant all that, but if He were the Messiah, He would have done what the Messiah is supposed to do. Why didn't He put an end to our troubles and really bring in the messianic age? Actually, things got worse for us after He came than they were before.

Josh: I can understand that. Can you go far enough to think that if He *were* the Messiah and you failed to believe Him that things would naturally turn sour for your people?

Nick: I suppose so, but I'm not ready to think of Him as Messiah at all. The Old Testament just doesn't say anything about the Messiah that Jesus could fulfill.

(With the biblical Jew, this objection comes up sooner or later. He has been taught about the trium-

phant advent of the Lord—Isaiah 9:6, "Unto us a
child is born, . . . a son is given"—and he is aware that
the Messiah will at last free the Jews from all their
troubles. He doesn't appreciate, however, the "suffer-
ing Servant" portions of the Bible, and here is where
it is necessary to educate the man, as Jesus did with
Nicodemus.)

Josh: The truth is, the Old Testament says the Messiah was going to suffer and die as an interces-
sor for His people. He was to be a sacrifice for
sin.

Nick: That sounds like the New Testament to me.

Josh: Can we look at the book of Isaiah together?
The fifty-third chapter describes the Messiah's
sacrificial ministry very completely.

Nick: Oh, come on! Don't start bringing out your
Christian interpretations of the Scriptures.
They are very hard to understand and I doubt
if we're going to find anything like what you're
looking for.

Josh: You don't mean to tell me you don't want to
look at your own Bible?!

Nick: O.K., bring it out.

The biblical Jew will not, in the end, avoid the

Scriptures. But he will say, even after a reading of so potent a chapter as Isaiah 53—which we outlined in chapter 4—that the Scripture is too subtle and needs a Rabbi's interpretation. Don't expect him to fall on his knees after you've finished a reading of that one chapter. Instead, he will find any number of objections to the most minute clause to escape seeing Jesus in Isaiah's writing. You need not debate these minor points. Rest your case because despite what he says, he will have seen the Word of God and he will remember. Many people don't appreciate that the Jew is a "covered up" character when it comes to religion. He doesn't show his reactions and thus the evangelist thinks he is getting nowhere. It's not true. Get out the "two-edged sword" and use it. Your Jewish friend, if you have cultivated him properly, will follow every word and will realize just as clearly as you do the implications of the Scriptures.

The dialogue with the biblical or orthodox (usually) Jew may take a different form. You may approach him instead about sacrifices, rather than prophecy.

Josh: Nick, you don't do sacrifices anymore, of course, since you don't have the Temple of God in Jerusalem. How do you expect to get redemption from your sins?

Nick: Well, I don't suppose God is charging me for my sins in the same way these days. He very well knows we have no Temple and no sacrifices.

Josh: Then God has changed His mind? You mean all He said in the Old Testament about "I have given you the blood for remission of sins" is no longer in effect?

Nick: Well, what can we do? That's just the fact of the matter. It certainly wasn't our fault the Temple was destroyed. You folks did that to us.

Josh: Well, the Roman folks did that to you. Us folks would rather see you subscribe again to God's principles about blood sacrifices. And, of course, we are offering the blood sacrifice of Jesus.

Nick: Well, for that I have to believe the whole story about Jesus, and I have to swallow the fact that all you Christians represent the people God loves.

Josh: Now you're getting it!

Nick: Josh, I like you and I respect you. I know your religion means a lot to you, and you're one Christian who demonstrates some real faith to me. I can believe that God has forgiven your sins, but, for goodness sake—all those persecutions down through the ages, all that hatred that we still see—were those your "saved" people?

103

(This objection will come up consistently and can only be answered truthfully from the gospel.)

Josh: The Lord said you'd know his disciples by their love. He told His men, "Love your enemies." When you see persecution, you are certainly not seeing genuine Christians.

Nick: Look, every year on the Day of Atonement I go to the synagogue and confess my sins. God Himself knows that's the only redemption available to me right now.

Josh: But if your atonement were already granted, wouldn't you want to accept that?

Nick: I certainly would, but how is it possible?

Josh: Do you remember Jesus' words on the cross, "It is finished"? He really meant that all men's sins were paid in full by His blood. He picked up the cup of redemption at Passover, "And as they were eating, Jesus took bread, and blessed it, and brake it, and gave it to the disciples, and said, Take, eat; this is my body. And he took the cup, and gave thanks, and gave it to them, saying, Drink ye all of it; For this is my blood of the new testament, which is shed for many for the remission of sins" (Matt. 26:26-28). You still drink that cup of redemption every Passover, don't you? And you still eat the unleavened bread with it, in the same manner that we Christians take communion.

Nick: Yes, but—

And so the objections will go on, but here Josh has told Nick some hard-hitting facts about blood sacrifice that tie together the Old and New Testaments. Without a doubt, Nick, very well aware of his Old Testament heritage—a Jew who keeps Atonement and Passover—has been moved to think. He may wander off somewhere during this dialogue, just as Nicodemus disappears somewhere during the teaching of the Lord in John 3, but he surely will remember.

The dialogues with Nick might continue in discussing the supernatural life experienced by Josh. Josh can cite the miracles he has seen, the answers to prayer he has had—and in this way make Nick "jealous," as Paul advised (Rom. 11:11). Nick will come to envy the prayer life and the personal God of Josh, if the latter is tactful and respectful about it. It's certainly of no use and quite antiscriptural to boast about salvation ("the free gift of God, lest any man should boast"). Nevertheless, what Josh has will increasingly interest Nick.

Be aware that bringing the Jew to the Lord biblically can be a lengthy process, calling on much knowledge and much patience. In our next section, we'll confront the Samaritan type of Jew found in much greater numbers today. There, a more simple and straightforward witness, rather like the famous Four Spiritual Laws, may be found very effective.

The Samaritan Objection

Talking to the "Samaritan" Jew of today—the liberal whose knowledge of spiritual things is only vague —requires a different sort of approach. One nearly has to put the Bible away when confronting a reform Jew, or a liberal conservative.

We witness to this sort of Jew in the same way we would witness to a lost liberal Protestant or Roman Catholic. We assume that any Bible knowledge to be found in the person will be quite simplistic and minimal.

We may very well have to begin with discussing whether God exists. The creation/evolution argument leads into snares and tangles but may have to be a starting point.

We'll call you "Josh" again, and we'll name our Samaritan Jew "Sam":

Josh: Sam, do you believe there is a God?

Sam: That's something we can't know, Josh.

Josh: Well, looking at the creation—all of this beauty and order, the wild flowers, the butterflies, the whole universe and how it works so well mechanically—does it seem like an accident?

Sam: I don't know.

107

Josh: If there were an intelligent Creator, Sam, would you want to know Him? Would you want to make contact?

Sam: Of course I would, but there is no way of knowing if He exists.

(Here, the Christian can proceed, if he is knowledgeable, into the good reasons why the world and its human beings suggest an intelligent Creator. Or, he might just go into his testimony of what he has gained, pursuing the opinion that God exists and that He can be gotten in touch with. Depending on the intellectual level and personal predispositions of Sam, you must decide on some way of approaching the idea of God. Let's suppose, as we continue, that we have at least gotten Sam to consider the possibility of God's existence.

Josh: O.K., so God exists and He made this whole world and everything in it. That means He made you and me. Do you suppose, now, that He cares about what happens to us?

Sam: I don't know.

Josh: Well, He made us in the same mold, so to speak, but with different ideas, different jobs to do, different lives entirely. We seem to reflect His creation in different ways. If you yourself had made a working model of a world with living things in it, wouldn't you care how it progresses? Look at how the gardener cares for his plants and his flowers.

Sam: Alright, I suppose that if we're going to agree that there's a God, He must care about how things progress in His creation.

Josh: Alright, let's consider His position about good and evil. Obviously, if we're to accept that He created the world and called it "good," He is interested in His supreme creation—man—being a fitting representative of what he made. Obviously, He is grieved when one man kills another man.

Sam: Alright, I'll buy that. But men kill each other all the time; even Christians and Jews.

Josh: True. So God is saddled with a problem. He made a creature of free will who goes out and does evil. What can be done about it?

Sam: I don't know; I'm not God.

Josh: Well, I know what can be done about it because I've read God's Book. He has written out what He wishes to do about the situation of sin and redemption.

Sam: Well, we don't know that God wrote the Bible.

Maybe it was just the writings of a bunch of old sages. Jewish people are pretty good writers.

Josh: Well, if you can assume with me that the Bible is an unusual book, I think it would be worth our while to look into it; at least, in its broad principles. After all, here is a book that has been a best seller for thousands of years. It has prophecy that some people seem to think comes out 100 percent. And it has moral lessons that all the world has profited by.

Sam: O.K., it's a good book. But what does it say about the good and evil?

It's not difficult to reach this point with the liberal Jew. He will ordinarily grant the Bible a special status among books, though he is uncomfortable actually opening the Word and reading the Scriptures. If you proceed through God's plan of redemption in very simple terms—man has sinned; God has provided a payment for that sin; God and man can be reconciled —you'll have an interested listener.

A more direct method with the liberal of any stripe is to talk about sin itself; without reference to God's plan. If he's a human being, he sins and he hurts about it. That sort of dialogue might go like this:

Josh: Are you ever depressed about your own behavior? Do you ever do things you really don't want to do?

Sam: Of course I do. I'm human, after all.

Josh: I'll tell you the truth, Sam—and you know me very well—I am not that troubled anymore. Ever since I began reading the Bible and praying to God, my sins have been falling away and I don't feel depressed about what's left of them.

Sam: Well, I'm glad it works for you. But my troubles might be just a little harder to handle.

Josh: Well, if there really is a God who made you, don't you suppose He can handle them?

There is no man anywhere unconscious of his sins, and every Jew and Gentile is looking for the solution. A straightforward presentation of the cross and its efficacy will go far toward relieving that inner pain of the heart. Even if the liberal thinks you're a religion freak, the intensity of his personal trouble with sin will cause him to listen and remember.

Prayer

We could go on and on with sample dialogues on how to witness to the Jews, but I think by this time you get the idea. You'll find your Jewish friends willing to listen as long as you have cultivated the proper fellowship. And your own inspirations as you look into the eyes of the person will guide you.

The most important dialogue, however, is with God. Nobody ever gets argued into the Kingdom;

God calls people into salvation. We must ask God, in every individual case, for His power to witness and for His calling of the unsaved one.

Prayer for the Jew is no different than prayer for the Gentile or any other kind of prayer. The book of James says simply, "Ye have not, because ye ask not" (Jas. 4:2). We must certainly remember to ask on behalf of the Jews.

The psalm bids us, "Pray for the peace of Jerusalem" (Ps. 122:6). True peace will come to Jerusalem, of course, when the Prince of Peace returns, but in the meanwhile let us feed the hungry as He told us to do. The irony that the original people to whom the Lord came are not being saved is something that should be straightened out at once. With a little knowledge and a lot of help from God—achieved through sincere prayer—the situation can be rectified.

Even with these sample dialogues, it's impossible to learn to talk to the Jew without getting some experience. Go at once; certainly you have a Jewish friend on whom you can practice. If it's necessary, just say, "Jerry, I need to practice witnessing to the Jews. Do you mind sitting there and giving me every objection you can think of to what I say?"

In my experience with Jewish evangelism, I have heard many people come forward and say, "Just last Wednesday, I prayed that God would bring me in touch with a Jew who was open, and last night I brought my dentist to Christ." Ask God for the opportunity; ask Him right now. You may have your chance to practice before you finish this book.

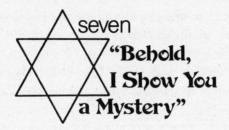

seven
"Behold, I Show You a Mystery"

Some of my best friends are Christians and they feel free to ask me all sorts of questions about my people. Christians are mystified by the Jews; they're not certain how to witness to the Jews or even how to get along with them.

In the spirit of clearing up some of those mysteries I will now present a few of the typical questions that come up, along with some answers. Perhaps the mystery will become less mysterious.

First, though, permit me a brief review of our foregoing chapters.

One More Time

If you'll bear with me I want to review the basic

methods of witnessing to the Jewish people which I presented in the earlier chapters. This has been a book of diverse topics, really, since the witness to the Jews requires at least a working knowledge of their long history, myriad traditions and peculiar culture of today.

We have, of necessity, talked about the entire development of the chosen people as we have it in the biblical record, their natural right to the gospel of Jesus Christ and their ways of being Jewish in the modern world.

Interspersed with all that was the three-point idea of witnessing to these remarkable people. I don't want this idea to get lost in the complications. So, let me repeat the name of my friend's church—FELLOWSHIP BIBLE CHURCH—since it presents our three basic methods in their proper order, and let me go over them lightly just once more.

In chapter 3 we talked about fellowship, our initial step. Fellowship is vital in witnessing to anyone, of course, but it is particularly important in dealing with the Jew. Due to the past abuses of Jews in general by the professing church and the Gentiles of the world, friendship must be restored if there is to be any meaningful communication today. And it must be genuine; the Jew is sensitive and has learned to be wary of all Gentiles.

Remember the Jews are "a peculiar people," in God's words, but not from outer space. They are neither superior nor inferior human beings—not to be regarded as some kind of religious royalty and not to

be snubbed by the country-club mentality either.

The self-congratulatory attitude of some churches that omit the witness to the Jews altogether is anathema. Remember, the Lord pointed out that even sinners can love their friends (see Luke 6:32, and big deal!). The witness to the Jews is surely God's will (Gen. 12:3; Rom. 1:16; 10:1; 11:1; Eph. 2:14, all of the book of Hebrews, etc., etc.). Christians who are not conscious of this important mission are just skipping over part of God's will.

Remember that the Jew is gregarious; he likes to talk. Remember that he's been warned—mostly against cults, but very well warned against the true church as well. Keep in mind that many Jews fear that coming to the Messiah will cause them to be no longer Jewish, and they will be considered a traitor in the Jewish community.

Keep in mind the Lord's command to love all men.

The Bible, our second step, we discussed in chapter 4. We considered the various categories of Jewish religion and how each might respond to your opening the Word. In general we concluded that the orthodox Jews might be the most amenable to studying the Bible with you, the conservative less so and the reform least of all. But we also noted the peculiarity of the reform to be open-minded "modern" intellectuals, perhaps more willing to look at your *New* Testament. We reached no hard and fast conclusions; each Jewish person is an individual case with the Bible.

In that same chapter, we discussed some Scripture that has been helpful in the mission work to the Jews as well as some sources where you can get complete information on this approach. The several dynamic missions to the Jews in this country can all supply any willing worker for Christ with biblical material he needs to approach the Jews.

In taking the Jew to church, our last method of witness that we covered in chapter 5, we discussed what sort of church might most appeal to the Jew. We pointed out that the special-events theory, where the Jew is brought to church because the church has prepared some special program of interest to the Jew, is not the best time to invite him to your church. The best way is that the invitation naturally follow from the fellowship and biblical discussions already initiated in your relationship with your Jewish friend.

We know from Scripture that the church is supposed to make the Jew jealous (Rom. 11:11), and we realize that what we want to show him is sincere worship, sincere fellowship and true honoring of God. We discussed the problems of the handshakers and the overeager evangelists who, with all good intentions, might really spoil things.

We talked about praying with the Jew and how acceptable it usually is to the Jew. Prayer is something all true worshipers of God have in common.

All in all, the three processes ask a great deal of *you*. You are required, if you are to witness to your Jewish friends successfully, to be sensitive, knowledgeable and patient. You will be taking on quite a job if you make this important mission a part of your service of Christ.

But you will be able to claim God's wonderful promise to Abraham, "I will bless them that bless thee."

"Funny, You Don't Look Christian"

People naturally ask me a lot of questions in church. Obviously I don't look like your typical Christian, since your typical Christian has been Gentile almost since the ascension, and I attract some notice. And then again I appear *very* Jewish and thus I am assumed to be *very* wise indeed (part of the "outer space" theory of categorizing the Jews).

I get a lot of letters in response to my arcane books (for some of the nastier letters I get see *Jews and Jesus*, Moody Press, 1977). It might serve well if I try to anticipate some of your questions as I conclude this particular book and I might save you writing a letter. Since my letters come from Jews, Christians and otherwise, my answers below will address everybody as best I can.

First, a few quickies—some answers for the Jews who will take exception to a lot of things I've said:

No, I'm not anti-Semitic, a Nazi or a Palestinian.

No, the goyim aren't using me or paying me off. I'm doing what God leads me to do.

Yes, I truly believe. I think Yeshua was our Man. This would be an awful life to live if I didn't believe.

No, I didn't marry a Gentile. She's a Christian.

Yes, my family thinks I'm crazy. No, they haven't held a funeral for me.

That done, let me proceed to some more general questions that typically come up:

Q. What percentage of Jews believe in Christ?
A. One percent is the usual figure given.

Q. Is modern Israel really a Jewish nation in the sense of keeping the Jewish laws and worshiping God in the Jewish manner?
A. Israel is a Jewish nation like America is a Christian nation.

Q. Do you do anything differently as a Jewish Christian from the rest of the church?
A. I like corned beef better than ham, and I take every opportunity to witness to the Jews. Otherwise I live just like a "real" Christian.

Q. Why are Jews so hard to save?
A. They're not. God does it all the time. Considering the rather lethargic efforts, on the part of His people, to witness to the Jews, God is actually doing pretty well. As we said, about one percent of all Jews are Christians, according to the Jewish figures on this. I wonder if one percent of all Gentiles are Christians.

Jews have a tremendous community spirit which they feel would be ruined by assimilation into Christianity. Although the average Jew doesn't practice anything even vaguely resembling biblical Judaism, he feels that he would lose his Jewish identity, for the Jewish community tends to take it very amiss when one of their number "goes over to the enemy." If the saved Jew practices a vital Christianity, he is invariably considered a troublemaker in the community (the case of Jesus Himself is a good example).

Basically the Jews are hard to save for the same reason that the Gentiles are hard to save. They simply don't know what the Bride is, and we haven't told them.

With the Jews this is a serious problem. Since they have no way of appreciating the true church, they confuse it with apostate churches and with Gentiles who have persecuted the Jewish people. My father thought Hitler was a Christian. You can imagine what he thought when someone suggested that he become a Christian too.

This confusion in the mind of the Jew over what a true Christian is promotes real antagonism. If any group of Gentiles who characterize themselves as "the church" become God's representatives, the Jew loses interest in Christianity pretty quickly. If I believed that the Popes, the Inquisitors, the Nazis (who wore the inscription "God is with us" on their belt buckles) and the people down at the local country club who won't let Jews in were all the true church, I would never have come to the Lord.

As it happened in my case, one Christian took the trouble to witness to me once in my life and I was saved immediately.

Q. Do you support Israel?
A. Certainly. As a Jew, Israel is my homeland. I'm going to make at least 1,000 trips there in the Millennium to come (see Zech. 14:16) or, more probably, actually live there with my Husband and King.

I definitely support the idea of Jews occupying Israel, which is a marvelous fulfillment of much prophecy. As a Christian I honor the chosen people in response to God's will (see Gen. 12:3; Rom. 1:16; Rom. 10:1; Rom. 11:1; etc.).

As an American I support the presence of any democracy in the eastern world. As a believer in God I deplore the progress of atheism in the form of communism, and I laud the presence of the Jewish people in the Holy Land as they continue to stem the tide. They have always been the stumbling block of tyranny and they courageously continue in this vital mission today. Uniquely, the nations of the world continue to be blessed by little Israel.

Q. My daughter wants to marry a Jewish boy. What should I do?
A. I assume you mean an unsaved Jewish boy. Don't commit suicide; my father-in-law survived the same problem.

If your daughter is a witnessing Christian of any skill at all she ought to be able to bring that young man to his Messiah. She's the best of all apostles in his case because he loves her.

Sit her down and appeal to her to witness, with all possible love and tenderness, and to delay the wedding in the hopes of her bridegroom's salvation. Pray. Treat the young man with all kindness and let the light shine through you so that he may see it.

If it all fails and your daughter wants to marry this unbeliever anyway, remind her of the sin she is committing and give her to the Lord. Don't harbor resentment; the young man may be saved later on through your steady good witness. The Lord may yet use the situation.

Finally your daughter's testimony is between her and the Lord. She has other sins. You have not prevented them all. Her Christian spirit and womanly wisdom will pervade her household, and her husband, who loves her, will duly note this.

In no case can you, as a follower of Christ, the forgiver of all sins, condemn your daughter or provoke her to anger. You must continue to copy the One who forgave His very crucifiers and took a common thief with Him to Paradise.

Job could not understand the terrible evils he suffered in his life, but he chose to trust God nevertheless, with good results.

This all should be applicable as well to the other case, the Christian boy and the unsaved Jewish girl, except that matters would be easier. The Christian man knows full well that he is in charge of his wife and his house and should sanctify them accordingly.

No one can oppose, of course, the marriage of a Hebrew *Christian* and a Gentile Christian on scriptural grounds. "There is neither Jew nor Greek in Christ." Such marriages, like my own, work out very well.

Q. What is the proper term for a saved Jew? Hebrew Christian? Messianic Jew?
A. "Christian," but the term has been ruined through the ages by pretenders. I prefer simply "believer." The Jewish people who followed Christ in the first

century called themselves *m'amim*, believers (see Acts 5:14).

Q. Will you get special consideration in heaven or the Kingdom because you are Jewish?
A. No.

Q. Why did you write this book?
A. To try to get you to help out with a little more of God's will. Thanks for reading it, but now it's high time you got cracking. Put the book down, get out of that chair and go see a Jew!

God go with you, brother and sister. Let us be able to say in the Kingdom together, "*am Yisroel chai!*"— The Jewish People Live!

Primary Scripture Passages for Witnessing to the Jew

The Messiah as the Enemy of Satan
  Genesis 3:15
The Messianic Promise to Abraham
  Genesis 22:15-18
Kingship of the Messiah
  Genesis 49:10; Numbers 24:17,18
Messiah as a Prophet
  Deuteronomy 18:18,19
Birth of Messiah
  Isaiah 7:14; Micah 5:2; Isaiah 9:6,7
Mission and Death of the Messiah
  Isaiah 53
Messiah's Resurrection
  Psalm 16:10; referred to by Peter, Acts 2:25-28
  Daniel 12:2,3; 1 Corinthians 15:22,23
The New Covenant
  Jeremiah 31:31-34; Hebrews 8:8-12
Salvation by Faith
  John 3:1-21; John 4:1-42